Secret Coastline

Secret Coastline

Journeys and Discoveries Along B.C.'s Shores

ANDREW SCOTT

Whitecap Books

Vancouver / Toronto

Edited by Elizabeth McLean
Proofread by Lisa Collins
Cover and interior design by Graham Sheard
Cover photographs by Andrew Scott

Printed and bound in Canada

CANADIAN CATALOGUING IN PUBLICATION DATA

Scott, Andrew, 1947-
    Secret coastline

    Includes index
    ISBN 1-55110-902-6

    1. Scott, Andrew 1947- —Journeys—British Columbia—Pacific
Coast. 2. Pacific Coast (B.C.)—Description and travel. 3. Pacific
Coast (B.C.)—Biography. I. Title.
FC3845.P2S36 2000   971.1'104   C00-910072-5
F1089.P2S36 2000

The publisher acknowledges the support of the Canada Council for the
Arts and the Cultural Services Branch of the Government of British
Columbia in making this publication possible. We acknowledge the
financial support of the Government of Canada through the Book
Publishing Industry Development Program for our publishing activities.

Contents

Acknowledgements

I'm grateful to the people who appear in these pages, for their kindnesses, the gifts of time they offered in response to my questions and needs. Many other people deserve thanks, as well—more people than I can list—for getting me places and helping me with all manner of things. This book could not have appeared without them. And I thank especially Katherine, the best of companions, who was with me on most of these journeys.

Coastal Map of British Columbia

Kincolith

Prince Rupert

Limestone I.

Ocean Falls

Klemtu

Bella Coola

Bella Bella

Hunter I.

Echo Bay

Port Hardy

Telegraph Cove

Jedediah I.

Kyuquot

Harwood I.

Merry I.

Gold R.

Sechelt

Flores I.

Vancouver

Ladner

Portland I.

0   50   100   150   200 Km

Foreword

IN 1997, after five years of writing a monthly column on ecotourism and never figuring out what the word meant exactly, I persuaded Beverley Sinclair, editor of the *Georgia Straight*, Vancouver's legendary weekly, to let me do something else. I wanted to write about where I lived and did the bulk of my wandering: the British Columbia coast. I had in mind a column that would explore B.C.'s coastal culture, glimpse its sacred places, feel the moods of its people, that kind of stuff.

The life of the coast, of course, is far too complex for any simple summing up. B.C.'s shoreline bears little resemblance to Canada's other ocean borders. There's so much of it for a start: 27 000 kilometres' worth if you go up every inlet and include all the islands. That's two-thirds of the way round the planet—a lot of room to hide in, or to find oneself. It's easy to get lost there. I wanted to call my column "Secret Coast," but it ended up with the name "Coastlines."

And that's a fine name for a column. "Coastlines" is only 840 words, plus a photo, each month (a steady job, so far). I thank Beverley and John Masters and John Burns at the *Straight* for allowing two-thirds of these stories to get a start in their pages. But if you ask me, those columns begged for more detail. And I've added it here. The book's chapters are twice as long as the columns—or longer. They have been redeveloped, updated, expanded. I've done the same with other stories, too, that originally appeared in *Vancouver, Western Living, Beautiful B.C., Waters* and *Discovery.*

Thirty chapters later, I've come to realize that this book is more like a series of postcards that have escaped their boundaries and grown together, interlinking, overlapping, sprouting voices, histories and herstories. This is one great place, they say. See it if you get a chance. The stories are a pastiche of coastal life, though there are not enough of them, of course, to do true justice to the terrain. Too many places and people and vocations are missing. Put these thirty together and what do you have? An exploration? Perhaps. A representation? I don't think so. A medley is more like it, a patchwork made with thirty pieces of cloth. I hope it keeps you warm for a few nights. (Quilting is extra.)

A surprising number of these journeys involve travel by kayak and nights in a tent. This is not because I wanted in any way to sound romantic or extol the joys of rusticity. I love hotels and hot showers. But I needed a boat to explore the coast, and a kayak was what I could afford. A kayak is the simplest and yet most complex way of travelling (only a true adept, it is said, perfects the art of packing and repacking). Sometimes uncomfortable but rarely scary, kayaking repays its habitués with amazing views of the coast, both close-up and wide-angle at the same time.

Faces of the Coast

THESE INDIVIDUALS INSPIRE me, and that is why I choose to write about them. I'm struck by how well their lives bridge the past and the future. All are firmly rooted in the traditions and heritage of the coast and yet, at the same time, all have truly creative and positive attitudes towards the future.

Stewart Marshall, for instance, uses an ancient means of travel to help him craft a fresh vision of the coastal landscape. Alexandra Morton and Jennifer Lash have discovered that to safeguard and deeply observe our marine environment, they must embrace a rural style of life that is fast disappearing from our shores. In the ultramodern home designs of Mark Osburn and Wayne Clarke one finds the beauty and utility of past dwellings. Peter Schmidt's wood sculptures recapture the glory of our oldest living beings. And Margaret Joe Dixon and her compatriots are reviving a threatened language in order to invigorate future generations.

These people are gloriously grounded in the present. They remind me that what's done is done, that there is no point in dwelling in the past. But their examples also tell me to learn from my mistakes, to try to hold on to what is best about our history and culture, and to celebrate what we have today.

Stewart Marshall

WE ARRANGE TO MEET on a mid-August Monday morning at Prince Rupert's public dock. Stewart Marshall will be paddling down from Alice Arm, further north on the B.C. coast. He's been staying there in an old cabin, finishing off some paintings begun earlier in the summer during a long, solo kayak journey along the eastern shorelines of Banks and Aristazabal islands.

I go down to the wharf on Sunday night, just to check things out. There among the motorboats and fishing vessels is a gleaming, wooden, handmade kayak, a huge thing—seven metres long and one metre wide—complete with fold-down mast and solar panel. Beside it, a muscular figure, burnt almost black by the sun, emerges from the confusion of bags and containers spread out on the float and greets me warmly.

"You got all that stuff in there?" a passing mariner asks him in amazement.

"Yup, and there's plenty of space left," Marshall replies.

"Well, how about coming over and sorting out my boat for me?" says the sailor, only half in jest.

By the next day, after more sorting and packing, his

Artist Stewart Marshall works outdoors and carries watercolour paints, brushes and paper in his ocean-going kayak. (ANDREW SCOTT)

great kayak and my conventional one are both ready for the open seas. We leave Rupert harbour by the northern channel, past the Tsimshian village of Metlakatla and the airport on Digby Island, and head out into Chatham Sound. I've been looking forward to this expedition for months. I have spent time with Marshall in Vancouver; in Sointula, a Finnish fishing village on Malcolm Island off B.C.'s central coast, where he lives; and in Maui, where he often winters. But I've never kayaked with him. And kayaking is what this fifty-five-year-old artist does as expertly as anyone in the world.

Stewart Marshall's life revolves around art, small boats and the wilderness—in that order. He has been painting since childhood days in Montreal. After high school, in order to finance art college, he spent a year as a trapper in northern Quebec, an experience that deepened his love of the wild. He worked as a graphic artist in Montreal in his early twenties, then set off in itinerant fashion to explore and paint in South America, India, Europe, the South Pacific and—again and again—on the B.C. coast. Although Vancouver's prestigious Bau-Xi Gallery has exhibited his work (as have many smaller galleries), he sells mainly by word of mouth and through an agent. He has a waiting list of buyers and strong followings in Hawaii and B.C.

"Stewart has a very sensitive viewpoint," says Lynn Shue, of Lahaina's Village Gallery on Maui. "You get the feeling that he really loves whatever it is he's looking at." The Bau-Xi's Xisa Wong agrees. "He's on such intimate terms with the coast," she says. "Nobody paints the spirit of the place better than Stewart. Technically, he's superb. He does a very good job of expressing the ethereal qualities and the strengths of the West Coast." But, adds Wong, somewhat wistfully: "He doesn't want to play the role of the artist to the role of the gallery. Some artists are just too independent."

As a boy growing up in the riverside suburb of Verdun, Marshall was bitten early by the small-boat bug, which has been known to get under people's skins and infect them forever. He has sailed solo across the Pacific, single-handedly exploring the huge reaches of Polynesia and painting scenes of island life from a sailboat. But it is paddling that he has refined to a high art. Marshall built his first kayak in the Gulf Islands a quarter-century ago; since then he has studied boat design, investigating the different types of kayaks and sealskin baidarkas used by Native people in the North, and constructed several vessels. His current expedition kayak, the one I admired at Prince Rupert, is lovingly crafted from cedar, pine, yew and fibreglass, and custom equipped with three sails, compass, rudder, global positioning system, solar-powered battery and running lights. It's big enough to sleep in and extraordinarily seaworthy.

Marshall's nautical skills are legendary. Each summer he paddles north on voyages hundreds of kilometres long (one year he logged 2000 kilometres on a trip to Alaska and back), living off land and sea, his stock of watercolour paper, paints and brushes carefully wrapped and protected against the elements. His paintings are impressions of the wildest and most inaccessible places on the B.C. coast: capes and coves seen in all kinds of weather from the vantage point of his tiny vessel; beaches and shorelines where he has grilled his catch of the day and camped under a tarpaulin.

Our goal this August day, however, is to camp at Lucy Island, site of an automated light station in the middle of Chatham Sound, a mere twenty kilometres from Prince Rupert. For me, even this will be quite a paddle. Fortunately, the day is sunny and calm. We take things slowly and do some fishing along the way. I'm in luck. I catch a pretty little pink salmon, perfect for supper, but when I relax my attention for a second, the cunning beast jumps out of the kayak back into the water.

"They're smarter than you think," is Marshall's only comment.

Lucy is a blaze of sunset when we arrive. Marshall, who has never been here before, scans the rocky shoreline, where waves crash against cliffs beneath the lighthouse tower, once manned but now desolate. We'll probably find a better landing spot on the other side of the main island, he says. The landscape looks inhospitable to me. We paddle round to Lucy's back door and enter an enchanted realm of islets and lagoons connected by white sand beaches and topped by wind-gnarled trees and bushes.

Next morning we awake in paradise: a peaceful, cloudless dawn; ancient conifers towering above; no human beings for many kilometres. It doesn't get better than this, so we decide to stay for a few days. After setting up a proper camp and breakfasting on porridge and fruit, Marshall introduces me to a new delight: fresh sea urchin roe. The only other time I've tried it, on sushi in Vancouver, I found it gamey and rather disgusting. But right out of the water like this, the roe is light and airy as mousse, sweet and delicious. Solid protein, too: a great little pick-me-up.

"If you go out at low tide with a stick or a net," says Marshall, "there's always something." Over the next two days, we sample crab, sea cucumber, cockles and clams. We steam tender fronds of kelp with our rice. And the pièce de résistance: filets of freshly caught rock cod and flounder fried in sea-urchin-roe batter. This is better than I usually eat in town. On his months-long trips, the only foods Marshall takes are rice, oats, flour, cornmeal, sugar, coffee and oil. And water, of course.

The fair weather continues, so Marshall sets the tools of his trade out underneath his tarp and prepares to work. He shows me some of the paintings he has completed over the summer. There are powerful seascapes: one under threatening skies; another at dawn, with delicate veils of purple mist rising over a clutch of islands; a third in orange, capturing the weird atmospheric effects created by the smoky pall of a huge forest fire. A few works include a human element: old cabins at Alice Arm, a derelict boat and pilings at Bella Coola. Others strip the coastal scenery almost bare, revealing the heart and essence of a remote natural world.

One piece, a swirl of indigo and violet with a muffled figure in a tiny shell of a boat careening down the slope of an enormous cresting wave, reminds me of the thin edge that Marshall travels. This is his record of a stormy November night journey in Queen Charlotte Sound. With a broken rudder and a badly leaking front hatch, he just avoided being blown past Cape Scott and far out into the open Pacific. The painting's foam and spray, gleaming under the cold milky beams of a full moon, make the hairs rise on my arm. It's like being there.

Marshall regularly seems to risk everything for the sake of art. The last time I'd heard from him, he'd just finished paddling from Vancouver Island to Cape St. James in the Queen Charlottes, a 220-kilometre crossing of dangerous ocean that took ninety-six hours. Halfway across, he astonished the seasoned crew of a deep-sea Polish trawler. In all their years of fishing, they'd never seen such a small boat in such a precarious place. The year before, after a sudden storm blew up, he barely survived a capsize—his first in twenty-five years of kayaking—in the ice-cold waters of one of the narrow inlets leading towards Bella Coola. Small wonder that when a speedboat had to be delivered from Great Slave Lake in the Northwest Territories, down the Mackenzie River, then north to Resolute in the Canadian high Arctic—a journey of almost 4000 kilometres—it was Marshall who was asked to help get it there.

Paralytic shellfish poisoning (red tide), attacks by hornets, close encounters with grizzlies: you name it and Marshall has endured it. He has shared narrow channels with wide cruise ships in pea-soup fogs. He has spent countless cold nights in wet clothing, and been wakened in his kayak by the spoutings of a nearby grey whale. He has tweaked the tails of Triton and Neptune, the ocean gods, and lived to paint the story. If you ask him why, he just shrugs his shoulders. Danger is an inevitable consequence of his deliberate approach to painting and to life.

He withdraws into the wilderness to revel, as he puts it, "in the inarticulate, the nonverbal, the illogical." Marshall stalks his artistic vision as a hunter stalks a deer—alone, without interruption, away from the artificial excitements of civilization. "I share this wilderness with too many other beings to get very lonely," he says, when I question him about isolation. As if on cue, a raven, which has been edg-ing ever closer to our camp, makes its move, grabbing a dis-carded fish head and carrying it off to safety. The raven is joined by its mate, and they caw triumphantly, anticipating a gourmet meal. Suddenly, a great shadow glides towards their hiding place: a bald eagle, who'd rather steal than hunt, has spotted them. The eagle grabs the morsel of flesh and flies leisurely off, blithely ignoring the two disconsolate ravens, who follow and harass it, but to no avail.

There's another side to Stewart Marshall, too—an off-season side, if you like—more social and relaxed. When the cold sets in and the daylight hours shorten, Marshall paddles back to Sointula, to a close community of fisherfolk and artist friends he has lived among for years. There, he finishes the paintings started in the summer, makes editions of silkscreen prints and plays his mandolin. Each year, he tries to spend a few months in Maui, where his son, now in his late twenties, lives and works.

On our reluctant return to civilization, three harbour porpoises cross our path, coming within five metres of the kayaks. We make camp that evening on a small island within sight of Prince Rupert and poach a beautiful coho that Marshall caught on the way. Tomorrow I'll begin the long drive back to Vancouver, and Marshall will head out to test himself against the elements one more time. I wonder where and when our next meeting will take place. But that's the beauty of this friendship. There are no hooks or expectations. Just a call out of the blue and the possibility of adventure.

ALEXANDRA MORTON

ECHO BAY is a hole in the granite wall of Gilford Island, between Vancouver Island and mainland B.C. Within this sheltered cove, surrounded by the maze of channels and islands that clogs the south end of Queen Charlotte Strait, a small community has made a buoyant adaptation to maritime life. When I first visited Echo Bay a few summers ago, our boat pulled up to a float beside Jim and Christine O'Donnell's Ark Gallery, which bobbed gently on its log platform. Other vessels were moored to other floats, in front of other floathomes. Architectural eccentricities flourished: curved dormers, bizarrely angled roofs, doors to nowhere.

Behind this strange suburb, a ragged cliff provides the echo that gives the bay its name. On the other side of the cove, a general store and post office perch proudly on a large concrete pontoon, taking the concept of flotation to new heights. This foundation was towed all the way from Seattle, where it had once formed part of a notorious floating bridge across Lake Washington, most of which sank while being refurbished. The post office is not even named after Echo Bay. It commemorates Simoom Sound instead, a former location twelve kilometres away. At Echo Bay one has the pleasant sensation that the wheels of bureaucracy have ground to a halt.

Alexandra Morton's ID photos of dolphins and whales are helping scientists learn more about marine mammal behaviour. (NADENE EBEL)

Canadian and U.S. flags fly in front of the store, where plenty of fancy cabin cruisers tie up in summer to yet more floats. When we were there, their owners were parked in deck chairs, exchanging nautical tips and sipping cool drinks and getting their barbecues ready. Near the head of the bay, on what passes in these parts for flat ground, a government wharf leads to a grassy, postage stamp-sized provincial marine park and an elementary school, one of the last schools left in the province without road access. Close by is the well-tended clearing of the Proctor homestead.

It was to Echo Bay that Alexandra Morton came in 1984. She had first visited British Columbia four years earlier, an innocent twenty-three-year-old marine mammal researcher with a special interest in the mysterious field of animal communication. Before that, she'd lived in Los Angeles, where she became fascinated with the work of neurologist and author John Lilly. Lilly believed that human beings and dolphins might soon be talking to one another. He enjoyed a vogue in the 1970s, and Morton wrote to him and managed, on the strength of previous experience as an artist, to get hired to paint a dolphin mural in the hallway of his home. She then spent two years of Sundays as a volunteer, cataloguing boxes of audiotapes that documented Lilly's attempts to teach dolphins to speak English. It was a way for her to listen to the tapes. But it was the soundtracks of dolphins talking to *dolphins* that really intrigued Morton, and she stopped working for Lilly. Instead, she persuaded Marineland of the Pacific in Los Angeles to let her continue her dolphin studies there.

The oceanarium had killer whales, too. "They looked really boring," Morton recalls, fifteen years later. "They'd be floating there like a couple of old inner tubes. But then the female, Corky, had a baby, and I was asked to move my sound equipment and record the whales. The baby died, and the mother went through three days and nights of mourning." Eventually, Morton believes, the male orca helped the female recover. "I didn't sleep those three days, I was so moved. There was a crack in that door. I understood what was going on. I saw mourning and pain, healing and optimism. I never went back to the dolphins, other than to visit."

Morton has been fascinated by the natural world for as long as she can remember. As a little girl growing up in Connecticut, she had a particular love for reptiles. "I spent my whole childhood in the woods, in the swamps and ponds," she says, "and I had this terrible sense of dread that when I grew up I'd have to give that up." Fortunately, chimpanzee researcher Jane Goodall became prominent about that time, and the twelve-year-old Morton adopted her as a role model, seeing in Goodall's example the possibility of a future for herself as an animal researcher living in the wilds.

And this is what she has become. "I'm totally living my dream," she says. "If the twelve-year-old I was then had known where she was going, she'd be thrilled. If you're living your dream, I think you've been successful." Today, Alex Morton is a respected whale and dolphin researcher, artist, writer and photographer—and a committed, deeply involved environmentalist. Her tanned, freckled features and mane of dark hair are known to thousands around the world from television and film appearances. She has become a role model for young women herself. In fact, as I interview Morton one day in Stanley Park during one of her infrequent visits to Vancouver, a pair of teenaged girls see her, do a double take and stop. "Aren't you the Whale Lady?" one of them asks excitedly as they come closer. "We've seen you on TV. What you do is so neat."

The Whale Lady lives in an eighty-year-old former floathouse, now pulled up on a piece of land purchased from long-time Echo Bay resident Billy Proctor. The building was once home to Proctor's mother, Jae. It is small but comfortable, with a gleaming wood interior, colourful Native artwork, and speakers wired to a hydrophone, or underwater microphone, so Morton can listen in on passing marine mammals. She shares this cozy corner of the coast with her partner, Eric Nelson; their four-year-old daughter, Clio; a brown cat named Briny; Kelsey, a gentle golden retriever; and Mocha, a diminutive, squirming mongrel.

Her situation sounds idyllic, but her sojourn in the province has been marked by a deep tragedy. Soon after she first arrived in B.C., Alex met Robin Morton, a filmmaker who pioneered the underwater photography of killer whales. They married and had a son, Jarret, now eighteen, an engineering student at the University of British Columbia. In 1986, Robin died in a diving accident.

Everyone assumed Alex and Jarret would leave the region. But they stayed. It was the only way, says Alex, she could continue Robin's work.

Morton's research takes her out into the Broughton Archipelago, west of Echo Bay. She photographs killer whales, helping update the identification work begun by government biologist Michael Bigg, who died in 1990, and carried on by a group of dedicated researchers and scientists. She notes all aspects of marine mammal activity in her area, not only of orcas but also humpback and minke whales and Pacific white-sided dolphins. Her detailed observations have resulted in a slew of articles for magazines both scientific and popular, and in two books for young people: *Siwiti: A Whale's Story* and *In the Company of Whales: From the Diary of a Whale Watcher.* Her deepest interests, as always, concern killer whale "language" and any correlations she can discern between their communication and behaviour. In her attic office, thousands of orca clues are filed away on a computer.

If you look at Morton's list of publications, a not-so-subtle shift takes place about 1995: fewer stories on marine mammals, more and more with titles such as "Salmon Farming's Hidden Harm" and "Fish-Farming—Growing Too Fast?" Morton says she has noticed that wildlife researchers go through a sad but inevitable evolution: at first they write about the beloved creature they are studying; later they write, often with growing desperation, about the dangers that humanity poses to that creature and its ecosystem.

It was around 1995 that Morton noted a major decline in orca sightings in the archipelago, a fact she attributes to the underwater noisemakers used by the area's numerous aquaculture operators to scare away seals. Fish farming was not just affecting killer whales and seals. Open-pen farms were polluting the ocean with feces and antibiotics. They were introducing diseases to wild fish. Atlantic salmon were escaping and breeding in B.C. waters, with who knows what impact on native stocks. Feed for the farms came from a harmful trawling industry that strip-mined the South American sea floor. And the open pens were a tourist eyesore. Morton lent her voice to those demanding that aquaculture be restricted and that farmers move to a closed-tank rearing system.

The longer Alex Morton lives at Echo Bay, the wider her point of view becomes and the more she realizes that to protect whales at the top of the food chain, the entire chain needs protection. The most important link in the chain is the salmon, which resident killer whales and many other species, including our own, rely upon. Morton suggests that "if you really want to do something for whales, bring back the salmon." A major motivation, she says, for writing her recent book, *Heart of the Raincoast: A Life Story*, was the fact that the book's co-author and subject, Billy Proctor, inspired a group of forty people, virtually the entire population of Echo Bay, to build a community salmon hatchery and clean and restock seventeen local creeks. "Everyone who lives near a stream could be doing that," says Morton. "People have forgotten that we're top-level predators and that salmon are our prey."

Proctor, who was born in the region sixty-six years ago and worked most of his life as a commercial fisherman, became a mentor of sorts to Morton. His knowledge of the coast is prodigious. When she first met him, in 1984, Morton asked Proctor about orcas, thinking he might have an anecdote or two. What she got back, she remembers, was "data," reams of precise, detailed information. When he asked her to go deckhanding for him in 1988, Morton thought she hadn't heard right. But Proctor could see she needed help. "His dad had died when he was a little boy," she says, "and he and his mom were on this island alone, and people came and helped them out." She worked with Proctor for two of the best salmon years in recent memory and made enough to buy her floathouse, generator, stove and fridge. "Fishing with Billy," she writes, "was a ride into the soul of the coast."

Morton saw in Proctor a beacon of hope. One of the best-known and most respected fishermen in the region, he was nevertheless struck, Morton writes in her understated prose, "with self-imposed questions about the impact of his work." He had a good life and a nice home but all around him salmon stocks were crashing and streams were being destroyed by logging. Proctor was honest enough to accept that he was part of the problem and brave enough to change his attitudes—quite a transformation for a middle-aged man steeped in B.C.'s "grab-it-while-you-can" traditions of resource extraction. Though home-schooled and terrified of public speaking, Proctor began writing letters and holding forth at meetings. Soon he was sitting on resource management and environmental review boards, where he continues to argue for increased habitat restoration, tighter sportfishing regulations, more selective commercial fisheries and a ban on pesticide use.

Today, Morton is working on a book that she wants to call *Witness to a Passage of Whales*. "It's basically everything I know about whales," she says. She is "completely content," she claims, to remain in Echo Bay, though she admits to missing movie theatres and good telephone connections. "Right now," she reports, "I'm trying to organize a community garden in one of the old abandoned logging camps." Her involvement in civic affairs eats into her research and writing time, she knows, but is essential nonetheless. Echo Bay has shrunk from about one hundred people when she arrived to only forty. "I want my community to survive," she says. "I want that one-room school to keep going so my daughter can go there. There's only five kids in it now."

The best thing she has done, Morton feels, is to stay put in one place for sixteen years, observing, recording, measuring. The patterns in nature, the cycles and changes, can only be revealed with this type of devoted, long-term research. "I study anything that comes through here now," she says. "I've got a feel for the humpbacks, the minke whales. And I'm waiting for the killer whales to come back. I'm hoping that when I'm in my fifties I can get back to the sound/behaviour correlation, and I'll be coming at it from the perspective of someone who has been listening to whales for thirty years."

OSBURN & CLARKE

"WEIRD HOMES in weird places" is how architect Wayne Clarke once described the work of himself and partner Mark Osburn. Certainly, the first Osburn/Clarke house I saw was unusual. It's located on Hudson Island, in the Gulf Islands opposite Chemainus. Hudson is unique in that a grass landing strip, dating from the 1940s, runs its entire length. One of the ten flying families that own the island had hired Osburn and Clarke to build a cottage there. The pilot flew me over in his 1952 de Havilland Beaver, which he'd used to ferry most of the building materials to the site. Later, all the cottage furniture arrived the same way.

The building itself is a high-tech dream: propane appliances, rooftop solar panels, a 6000-litre buried cistern. But the design is pure 1920s nostalgia. An enormous buttressed Rumford fireplace made of sandstone from the beach dominates the living room and acts as a trombe wall or heat sink. Dormer windows light the upper floor, where three bedrooms are connected by a railed bridge resting on a long driftwood cypress log. Outside, an arbutus-shaded deck leads to a walkway that leads in turn to a smaller deck by the ocean.

It's a perfect home, I thought at the time, and I've wanted something similar ever since. For over a decade

The Cottage Kings:
Wayne Clarke,
left, and Mark
Osburn specialize
in architectural
designs for the
B.C. coast.
(COURTESY OSBURN/CLARKE
PRODUCTIONS)

now I've admired the designs of Osburn and Clarke, who specialize in recreational waterfront buildings. The pair have many admirers. They are, in fact, often referred to as the Cottage Kings.

If there is such a thing as a West Coast architectural style, then Osburn and Clarke have it. Their elegant, superbly crafted homes blend into the landscape and embrace the weather; comfortable and practical, they suit the realities of B.C. coastal life. The Osburn/Clarke style is inventive, but it manages to honour the past. Their houses are usually built of red cedar and Douglas fir; the interior structural elements are often left exposed. It's easy to catch in their airy, open designs a reflection of an old cannery building, a boat shed or an arrangement of boardwalks, docks and piers—even a Haida longhouse.

I first interviewed Mark Osburn in what seems an unlikely location—way out at the Coal Harbour end of Vancouver's Pender Street. A coastal business such as Osburn/Clarke Productions needs an urban base, though a highrise headquarters would never do. Instead, the partners choose to hang their slate where a fifty-year-old streetscape of two-storey buildings is tucked away beneath encroaching towers. Here, the buzz of floatplanes reminds a visitor that this cosmopolitan city still sits at the edge of wilderness.

If you open their nondescript front door, you'll be greeted by a giant fish with three bathers on its back. Rotate the fish's tail and the bathers move up and down. Other mechanical whimsies—a flamingo with paddlewheels, a pilot-operated duck—are suspended about the main office. These floating *objets d'art* give fair warning: the people who work here do things differently. There's the mysterious absence of computers, for instance. "They're not smart enough," Clarke once told a visiting reporter. The flying fetishes are his, made years ago for a book he researched and wrote about wind-driven folk art.

As we spoke, Osburn referred frequently to a map of B.C. hung on the wall behind his drafting table. A squadron of push-pins marked the company's projects on the west coast of Vancouver Island and around the Strait of Georgia. Ten years later, the pins clustered along the shores of the lower strait form an almost solid line. Large islands with household names, such as Pender, Bowen and Saltspring, are especially well furnished with the partners' work, but so are smaller, less familiar ones: Vargas, Balaklava, Hardy, Stuart, Hernando.

West Coast recreational housing evolved from the summer camps of the 1920s and 1930s, with their tents and rough shelters, to the rustic cottages of the 1950s, where mom supervised the kids in July and August and dad showed up on weekends. Over the next two decades, cottages grew fancier but were still mostly modest. Beginning in the 1980s, however, many older couples with grown-up children sold the family home in the city, bought a condominium and sank the balance into a substantial "country house," site of weekend getaways and family reunions.

Osburn and Clarke have known each other since the late 1960s, when both went to architecture school at the University of British Columbia. They first worked together at Expo 86, doing exhibit design for the B.C. and Canadian pavilions (the B.C. Revue and Boom Boat Ballet were their projects). After the fair they formed a business partnership. And business was good.

The partners, both family guys in their mid-fifties, are a good fit. Osburn is the gregarious one, with a deep feel for the B.C. coast, having grown up there and worked as a commercial fisherman before settling down as an architect. He looks after the initial stages of the project, "setting up the problem," as he puts it, "meeting with the client, handling the siting issues and dealing with the overall organization of the idea."

Clarke is the technician, albeit one with an acute visual sensibility. A military brat whose family moved all over, he is an engineer as well as an architect. He takes the idea and turns it into a finished design, determining how the house should be built, resolving its structural requirements, deciding on its final touches. "Every project is a collaborative effort," declares Osburn. "I start them and he finishes them." Three assistant architects handle the details. The firm takes on a mere twelve to twenty projects annually. "The way we do them, we can only do so many at a time. It is very much a custom service."

Many Osburn/Clarke designs are dictated by the site. "You like to know as much as you can about a site," muses Osburn. "And it has to be very specific information. We have a simple principle for siting: you find the best place on the property and then you put the house right around it." The partners may spend three days, in all types of weather, determining that place.

On one Vancouver Island property, for instance, a creek ran smack through the best place to build. Rather than alter the landscape and reroute the water, the partners designed a house on stilts with the creek flowing underneath it. For an Eagle Harbour home on an awkward, sloped West Vancouver lot, they put the building on a stonework pedestal. The view out the living room windows to a "negative-edge" pool is so well orchestrated that you can't tell where the pool stops and Howe Sound begins. The illusion of water-front living is complete, even though a road runs between the house and the sea. Steep slopes are a fact of life on the coast, and Osburn/Clarke designs are often cunningly can-tilevered so they appear to project over the water.

Many coastal homes must be constructed in exposed, weather-beaten locations. "When the rain comes horizontal-ly," reports Osburn, "walls have to be roofs." He and Clarke once designed a Bowen Island house for a south-facing piece of property that "took a lot of weather." The house was cre-ated as "a series of conditions that allows for less and less (or more and more) protection." There's a cozy hearth, a bay window with a view, a veranda under an overhang, another outside area behind a trellis, a patio sheltered by a shoulder of rock, and an extremely windy outer deck. The degree of exposure becomes a choice, not a constraint.

"Another factor that comes into play," says Osburn of house design, "has to do with the wonderful curiosity that occurs on the coast, where people bring their own ideas about what they want to do. That's part of the culture, I think, putting something you've brought with you into the wilderness."

A Pender Island home that won a Canadian Wood Council Award illustrates his point. The owners and their extended family had camped on the site in tents, in a small gazebo and on a communal deck under a huge sailcloth. The final design retains that sense of openness: the entire front and side of the house retracts like a set of gigantic sliding French doors and disappears into recesses in the walls, leaving the interior open to the elements. Sleeping areas are enclosed with moveable canvas partitions. The building is like a giant tent. "What the owners had done to live on the site temporarily," explains Osburn, "became the program for the house."

Another Wood Council award-winner, located on a tiny Gulf Island named Mowgli, took its "program" from an old log cabin on the property. The client wanted a new log cabin. He also wanted open, airy rooms. The two concepts were incompatible. The architects proposed post-and-beam construction with a nonbearing log "infill." They also introduced the client to the sport of beachcombing, which he took to with enthusiasm, bringing in bigger and bigger logs for use on the job. Finally, he dragged ashore a twenty-metre-long fir boomstick, which became a massive truss supporting one side of the cottage. To get materials onsite, a miniature marine ways had to be built, complete with a wheeled trolley.

Some of the buildings are in truly remote spots. One Osburn/Clarke design I visited—a private fishing lodge built on a tiny island at Kyuquot—required a ten-hour trip along the west coast of Vancouver Island on a coastal freighter, plus a paddle in a kayak. Kyuquot Lodge, which Osburn shares with twenty-odd friends and associates, is his hideaway, the place he can indulge his love of wilderness adventuring. He generally arrives by floatplane.

My favourite Osburn/Clarke project is one I've never visited, just fallen for from photographs. It's among their earliest and most cherished designs: a principal house, a guest house and a combination wood shed and workshop, all supported by a huge yellow-cedar platform and set in a grove of fir and arbutus. The location—Pasley Island in the gusty mouth of Howe Sound—is idyllic. Mark Osburn's family has a cottage in the area, and Pasley is home to several of the firm's structures.

This particular cluster of buildings seems timeless, at perfect peace with its surroundings. The influences— Oriental, Native American, nautical, industrial—merge and settle in the imagination and the soul. Bleached wood surfaces glow in the pearly coastal light. This place is getting better as it ages. The huge driftwood trusses and fireplace stones came right off the beach. The wood detailing and joinery are exquisite. And there's even a touch of whimsy: a model seaplane suspended from the open roof, its propeller serving as a fan.

MARGARET JOE DIXON & THE *TAʔAS*

THE MOM-AY-MON Nursery School occupies a modest prefab trailer on the Sechelt First Nation lands, next to Trail Bay on the Sunshine Coast. It's a cheerful place. Tiny chairs are set around low circular tables, and the walls are covered with bright posters and artworks. The children only come to class from Monday to Thursday. Friday is the day that staff catch up on administrative chores and prepare for next week's sessions. It's also the day that Lori Dixon has arranged for me to talk to the *taʔas*.

Taʔa means "granny" in *shashishalhem*, the Sechelt language. But senior *taʔa* Margaret Joe Dixon, who is Lori's mother-in-law, and junior *taʔa* Violet Jackson provide much more than grandmotherly affection to their charges. By teaching *shashishalhem* to impressionable preschoolers, they have become frontline workers in a vital campaign the Sechelt people are waging to pass their language on to succeeding generations and retain their cultural identity.

In the small nursery school office, I join Margaret Joe Dixon, Vi Jackson, teacher's aide Daphne Paul and nursery supervisor Lori Dixon, who was also elected one of the Sunshine Coast school district's seven public trustees in the 1999 municipal elections. Margaret Joe Dixon and Jackson are

Daphne Paul, left, and Lori Dixon stand behind Vi Jackson, left, and Margaret Joe Dixon at the Mom-Ay-Mon Nursery. (ANDREW SCOTT)

elders, part of a group of about twenty people, all over fifty-five, who are still reasonably fluent in their traditional language. Lori Dixon and Paul are members of a younger generation. They understand some of the language but cannot speak it.

Over the past decade, a program of language instruction has been gradually developed for Sechelt's elementary and secondary schools, and today over a hundred children in grades one to ten attend *shashishalhem* classes. And while many Sechelt First Nation members have made important contributions towards keeping the language alive, the origins of the teaching program can be found right here with Mom-Ay-Mon and Margaret Joe Dixon.

"She would complain and complain," recalls Lori Dixon. "She would say, 'When is council going to do something?' and 'All the old people will be dead before we start teaching the language to the kids.'" Finally, Lori's husband, Stan Dixon, a former chief and band councillor, suggested that

Margaret go up to the nursery and volunteer. "I taught her how to put together a little twenty-minute presentation," says Lori, "and she still uses it. Soon the kids were going home loving *ta?a* time at school.

"They were learning the names of the animals. They were counting and starting to sing. And they were going home with all this and saying things and the parents were amazed. So then the parents got excited and started showing up just to see what was going on." The Sechelt band started to pay Margaret for her time. Eventually, two *ta?as* were needed to keep up with the kids, who were "sopping up everything like sponges," according to Lori. The *ta?as* work together, jogging each other's memories and helping each other prepare new lessons.

Margaret, who has lived in Sechelt for over seventy years but was born at Tsonai, an important former village site far up Jervis Inlet at Deserted Bay, doesn't claim any credit for herself. "The elders have been working on the language with Ron Beaumont since 1970," she says, "and we're still coming up with new words." Twice a month for thirty years the Sechelt elders have gathered with retired University of British Columbia linguist Beaumont to preserve and record *shashishalhem*'s subtle complexity. This project, a remarkable testament to dedication, has already resulted in the publication of a grammar and teaching guide to the language. In four or five more years, Beaumont, who is now sixty-five, also hopes to publish a dictionary. "I only hope I live long enough to finish it," he says.

Shashishalhem is one of the Salishan family of languages spoken around the shores of Georgia Strait and Puget Sound and as far into the interior as the Okanagan. There are enclaves of Salishan speakers to the north at Bella Coola and to the south in Oregon. The Sechelt tongue is rich and expressive, with a very different sound system from English. Many English consonants—"b," "d," "f," "j" and "r," for instance—have no equivalents in Sechelt. And English has nothing like the Sechelt throat-catch, where a constriction at the back of the throat is followed by a sharp release of breath, or glottal stop. Linguists represent this sound with a symbol: the question mark without the period that we have already encountered in *ta?as*.

Some *shashishalhem* consonants—the "k" sound, especially— are produced at the back of the mouth and often "glottalized," or combined with a throat-catch. Others are "labialized," or pronounced with rounded lips and a "w" sound, as in "quit." There's the beautiful "lh" sound, produced by breathing past the edges of the tongue, as in the "thl" of "Kathleen," and the hissing "ts" in *stsekay*, or sockeye, a Sechelt word known to everyone in B.C. Sechelt speakers would recognize many of the words in other Salishan languages, such as Squamish or the Halkomelem spoken in the Fraser Valley, and would probably understand much of a neighbouring language such as Comox, spoken in the Powell River area directly north of Sechelt.

Sadly, despite the desperate efforts of a number of devoted people, the outlook for *shashishalhem* is precarious, as it is for several of B.C.'s thirty-three surviving First Nations languages. Some B.C. Native tongues are already extinct: Pentlatch, for instance, which was spoken on Texada Island and in the Parksville area of Vancouver Island, has disappeared forever. Many of the dwindling group of Sechelt elders acknowledge that it may be too late now for sufficient numbers of future generations to gain fluency in their ancestral language.

The elders rarely speak *shashishalhem* among themselves today. "It's hard," says Margaret Joe Dixon. "We've tried.

We're not too strict with it. We talk about it but we don't do it, just speak our language." Children may pick up a rudimentary knowledge of the language at school, but they have nowhere to practise it. Their parents don't speak it. The dominant culture—television, popular music, sports— reinforces English at every turn.

Donna August Joe, who has been another driving force in establishing Sechelt language programs in the school sys-tem, is well aware of the problems. One sunny afternoon I meet Joe and two of her fellow teachers, Valerie Bourne and Bernie Sound, at Sechelt's new Kinnikinnick elementary school. Here's another cheerful place. On the classroom walls are dozens of *shashishalhem* words and the things they represent: *sk'ík'ák'*, the crow; *shálshal*, the moon; *chéchím*, the fire. The kids are gone for the day, but they had been counting from one to five before I arrived: *tála, t'émshín, chálhás, mos, tsílachis.*

Joe and her colleagues have had to be creative in their approach to teaching. "There's very little funding available," she says. Resources are limited. There are no precedents for teachers to fall back on: First Nations language training is new territory, and those involved must come up with everything themselves. They cannot research lesson materials in the school library, for instance, or look them up in an encyclopedia. They cannot order Sechelt storybooks from the nearest educational supply store. To fill one of many gaps, Bernie Sound has produced a series of about twenty hand-lettered, photocopied readers, illustrated by a local First Nation artist.

The elementary school language program is deservedly popular. Nearly all the First Nation children attend, and plenty of non-Native youngsters are learning *shashishalhem*, too. Donna August Joe has also been working for several years to develop a curriculum for Chatelech secondary school, where Theresa Jeffries and Diane Joe teach the Sechelt language to about twenty-five older students. As yet, however, these classes are not accredited and cannot count towards graduation or university entrance.

Another difficulty facing Sechelt language teachers is the entrenched hostility that many First Nations members harbour towards the entire "western" education process. Standardized reading, writing and numeracy test results indicate that many of B.C.'s First Nations students are lagging far behind their non-Native classmates. The Sechelt First Nation's adult education programs have not been successful, either. "There are a lot of strong feelings around school," explains Lori Dixon. "Everyone treasures the idea, but there's a lot of negative emotion, too."

She and Margaret Joe Dixon trace these attitudes back to the residential schools, one of which operated in Sechelt from 1904 until the 1960s. The Catholic Oblate priests who ran the school tried to eradicate traditional customs and forbade students to speak their own language. "My husband and I never wanted to teach our children our language," says Margaret, "because we didn't want them to be punished when they went to school." Thus there is a direct link between the school and the slow death of the Sechelt language, which is unable to make the transition across generations of non-speakers.

Resentments towards school and authority have become deeply engrained. "We have a lot of anger that has no face and no name," Lori declares, "and it has filtered down even to the generation here." She gestures towards the nursery. "There's a lot of fear and a lot of anger and it all goes back to the residential school. That's why our children aren't doing well in school generally." For most of those who have been through the residential system, "school is something like an enemy," emphasizes Margaret.

To overcome these feelings is a constant struggle. Fortunately, the Sechelt are a resilient people with a progressive, optimistic outlook. Success stories are abundant. Many students do well at school and some have gone on to university and earned degrees, bringing valuable skills back to their community. All of the teachers and *ta?a* are working to make local school programs more relevant to First Nations students—a few of whom have become quite adept at *shashishalhem*. Most Sechelt members believe that even a little knowledge of the language will strengthen their young people's sense of identity and increase their understanding of the traditional culture.

"Today," says Margaret Joe Dixon, "our kids can talk to me as I'm passing by. 'Hi, *ta?a. Ku-á-chxw ?íy?*' they ask me. They ask me how I am in our language. That makes me feel proud."

PETER SCHMIDT

THE WORKING DAY starts early at Pink Whiskers—
before dawn on most mornings. Doug de St Croix stumbles
up the dock from the *Eljac*, the big old wooden boat he lives
on. Don Knight stumbles down from the cabin on the bluff,
which he shares with his partner, Pure. Peter Schmidt
brews a pot of tea in the main house. Theoretically, he lives
there alone, except for Jade and Zack, his dogs. But the
place always seems full of people, especially Dominic and
Cyrus, a friend's lively six-year-old twins, who often visit
on weekends.

After breakfast, the three men hike up to a clearing
where two open-sided studios shelter a collection of huge
red-cedar burls and stumps. Nearby is a portable sawmill.
Today the crew will be culling selected second-growth logs
from the property to provide operating capital for Schmidt's
new business: the making of "functional sculpture." As de
St Croix and Knight fire up the 'dozer and a recalcitrant
skidder, Schmidt shows visitors some work in progress. In
one studio, he has been slicing stumps lengthwise with the
1.5-metre blade of a heavy chainsaw. At the other, Knight
has been shaping the slices into benches with a power adze
designed specifically for the job.

Sculptor Peter Schmidt rests on an old-growth trunk similar to the ones he uses to fashion his monumental art works. (ANDREW SCOTT)

Schmidt owns seventeen hectares here on the shore of Agamemnon Channel, between the Sechelt Peninsula and Nelson Island. For his latest venture, he has been scouring the region's coastlines for big old-growth stumps, many of which find their way down rivers and streams to the ocean, where they end up decaying. Schmidt takes this wasted, cast-off wood and makes marvellous seats, tables and outdoor sculptures from what would otherwise be debris. Now he has a contract with landscape architect Jerry Vagelatos to provide the creative wood components for Surrey Memorial Hospital's new Children's Recovery Garden Courtyard.

Don Knight is Schmidt's assistant in the sculpture business. Doug de St Croix is helping out with the labour-intensive logging. Back at the house, Doug's girlfriend, Sarah Kelly, is at work setting up a Web site for Schmidt and computerizing his books. There's a communal air to the operation. The workers often eat together, for instance. "People come and go," says de St Croix. Friends and neigh-bours, part of the tight maritime community that inhabits this jumping-off point to the British Columbia coastal wilderness, drop by for coffee or a glass of homemade wine. The nearest centre is Egmont, twelve kilometres away, and that's just a tiny place.

The Pink Whiskers property got its name from the orig-inal homesteader, who apparently had a large red beard. It's halfway down Agamemnon and not accessible by car. Katherine and I kayak there from Earls Cove, the BC Ferries terminal at the north end of the Sechelt Peninsula. There is no public dock at the cove, and we have to get permission to wrestle our boats across private land just behind the terminal's fence.

After this excitement, the paddle in is simple. We pass strange, red-ochre pictographs painted on granite cliffs and are followed by harbour seals. A couple of coastal freighters, former drug-running boats confiscated and sold by the gov-ernment, are moored along the shore. Across the channel, off Nelson Island, rows of white Styrofoam floats mark numerous oysterculture leases. The water here is clean and calm, ideal for shellfish, and oysters from the area are justly celebrated. Every so often, a rustic home, complete with dock or boat ramp, peeks out from the forest.

Schmidt, who at forty-two has spent much of his working life as a fisherman and a logger, acquired his small kingdom eleven years ago. It had been a fish farm and hatchery; a substantial pier jutted into the bay there with a boatshed at one end and a bunkhouse at the other. Schmidt set up a mill, cut logs, expanded and modernized the buildings, and put in electricity and telephone lines. He earned a living milling lumber for his neighbours and then helping them construct docks and homes. He lived there with his girl-friend for eight years, but when the relationship fell apart and she moved out, he found himself living in the wilds alone, which he didn't like. Peter Schmidt needed people in his life, but he didn't want to leave. So with characteristic cheek, he decided to start his own community.

He was surprisingly well equipped for such an ambitious undertaking. Raised in a Metchosin commune and educated at a Saturna Island free school, he had built his first house, at sixteen, near Prince George, in an alternative community named Mudslide. Schmidt envisioned Pink Whiskers as a self-sustaining "ecovillage," owned by its members, who would run a retreat and ecotourism centre, manage an oyster lease, build boats, grow food, eat together and live in separate residences.

"I thought about this idea for a long time," he says. "I talked to hundreds of people and dragged dozens of them out here in search of co-investors. A whole variety of different people almost got involved. It looked like it was going to happen." He sank two years and thousands of dollars into the project, but in the end the move from city to wilderness proved too big a step for most people. "They had to come and join *my* plan," Schmidt admits. "We weren't a group of equal contemporaries with an idea, who then went out and implemented it, so the project couldn't initially be in balance."

Schmidt's fascination with construction and communities, combined with a background in logging, led him to his current enterprise. "I was never very interested in mainstream, building-inspector, vinyl-and-plastic construction," he says. "Legislated consumerism is what that is." Instead, he wanted to recycle salvaged materials. "I could build a beautiful house here, one that would last for 500 years, for about a thousand dollars in materials, plus labour. But we have things legislated so it's impossible to do that."

Inspired by a book by David Pearson called *Earth to Spirit: In Search of Natural Architecture* —and by Hilary Stewart's *Cedar: Tree of Life to the Northwest Coast Indians* —Schmidt began to craft architectural structures out of discarded bits of old-growth timber. "There's a terrific need," he claims, "for finding the wood's thousand-year-old beauty and bringing it to the people who most desperately need to see it." City dwellers, in other words— those who are cut off from the power of the natural world. He shows us photos of a massive cedar burl that wraps round a cedar bench and turns it into a throne fit for a forest deity. Hundreds of hours of labour have gone into smoothing and polishing the wood, which glows with an inner life and truly conveys the majesty of B.C.'s old-growth forests.

As a result of this monument and others like it, Schmidt gained the experience necessary to snag the Surrey hospital contract. The project calls for ten gnarled benches and six massive stump and burl sculptures, most of which sit semi-finished in his outdoor studios. Several form cavelike enclosures for kids to play in. Like all Schmidt's pieces, they make a strong environmental statement as well as being gorgeous and functional.

For the artist, these pieces are just the beginning. Schmidt is currently pitching a project to the community of Pender Harbour for an information centre made from an upside-down cedar stump cut into pie-shaped wedges arranged in a circle, with the roots suspending a roof. Stumphenge, he calls it. "I have this vision," he says, talking of another design, "of a sixty-foot cedar trunk, half standing, half on the ground in the form of a long, carved bench. A piece of art for an enormous public foyer." He wants to turn a cross-section of yet another old trunk into a gigantic thousand-year calendar.

So many ideas, so little time. Ironically, Schmidt may have to sell Pink Whiskers and move to Egmont or Pender Harbour as a result of his infatuation with sculpture. The isolation that nurtured his unique viewpoint is now hindering him from bringing his dreams to realization. His business needs road access: the sheer size of his creations presents daunting logistical problems come delivery time. But he'll do whatever he has to, he says, to share with others his awe and appreciation for the ancient evergreen beings that once dominated this landscape.

JENNIFER LASH

BENEATH THE CLEAR green waters off West Vancouver's Whytecliff Park, a red Irish lord cruises through a forest of white plumose anemones. Neon-orange sea stars and purple urchins decorate the ocean floor. Bright yellow nudibranchs (fancy ocean-going slugs) patrol the ledges. Marine fruits and vegetables grow there: sea lemons, sea peaches, sea cucumbers. Crevices are home to octopuses and crabs. Below a gap in the rocks, a pile of bleached bones signals the lair of a wolf eel. Don't stick your hand in there.

Whytecliff is diver heaven, a popular scuba training site and playground for local aquanauts. Despite its closeness to a busy ferry terminal, the underwater life is abundant, the result of a "no-take" policy that prohibits all fishing and gathering. Amazingly, there are only three no-take preserves—or "harvest refugia"—in Canada. All are small and near Vancouver.

Jennifer Lash, executive director of the Living Oceans Society, wants this situation to change. A growing number of people want more no-take zones established in B.C. Considering the high level of protection granted nearly 12 percent of the province's land base, it's surprising to learn that less than one-tenth of one percent of B.C.'s coastal waters are similarly shielded.

Living Oceans Society executive director Jennifer Lash is working to change our attitudes towards marine ecosystems. (CATHERINE LASH)

"Basically, that's because people don't see what's under there," says Lash, a keen diver. "And fish don't have fur. That's a big problem." The terrestrial protection strategy is successful because British Columbians love animals and trees. But most attempts at marine preservation start with sport divers, the only outdoor types to actually view the province's saltwater wealth. With over 7500 known species—and perhaps as many not yet identified—the ecosystems off our shorelines are as rich and exotic as any in the world.

Lash, thirty-six, has become a strong force in the move-ment to protect B.C.'s vulnerable underwater environment. Before joining Living Oceans, she served as marine campaign coordinator for BC Wild and executive director of the Marine Life Sanctuaries Society of B.C. "I've always been intrigued by the ocean," she says, a fascination that first drove her to Australia, where she became obsessed with scuba diving and snagged a dream job as a researcher at Australia's Great Barrier Reef—"an absolutely amazing experience."

Back home, Lash studied public policy and administration at an Ontario university, graduated, then blithely announced to parents and friends that she was "going off to save the ocean." She washed ashore at Nanaimo and worked as an abalone researcher at a federal biological station. As a volunteer, she joined a campaign to protect the living treasures of Gabriola Passage in the Gulf Islands. Eventually she quit her job to become a full-time eco-warrior and spearhead a lengthy—and as yet unfulfilled—effort to get the pass designated a no-take zone. Today she lives at Sointula on Malcolm Island, an activist fishing community on the central coast.

The Living Oceans Society grew out of a marine-awareness crusade started in 1995 by Earthlife Canada. Its mandate: to bring together all those with a stake in preserving the ocean—fishers, environmentalists, First Nations, scientists, outdoors enthusiasts, bureaucrats—to talk about what needs to be done. Two of the society's founders, Elliott Norse and Michael Soulé, are world-famous conservation biologists. Directors include reps from the Sierra Club, David Suzuki Foundation and United Fisherman and Allied Workers Union.

The members of Living Oceans are determined to prevent oil and gas exploration off the B.C. coast and to improve fish-farming practices. They want to coordinate with similar groups in the United States. Living Oceans is working with REEF (the Reef Environmental Education Foundation, based in Florida) on a worldwide project encouraging sport divers to monitor local sites and collect data on a volunteer basis. But the main initiative has always been to establish a network of protected marine zones in B.C.

Some safeguards are already in place. We have 104 areas and 529 000 hectares with various degrees of preservation: wildlife management zones, marine parks, ecological reserves. Ninety percent provide little ecosystem protection. Most marine parks are recreational, set aside as pleasant places for boaters to frolic. Many reserves protect only one species and allow activities that are dangerous to others. Whale watchers, for instance, are rightly excluded from Robson Bight in Johnstone Strait, where killer whales gather at "rubbing" beaches. As the watchers bob in tourist vessels just outside the reserve, their binoculars often bring into focus dozens of huge seiners merrily fishing in Robson Bight. In the entire province, only forty-six hectares of ocean are totally off-limits to harvesting.

Jennifer Lash has thought a lot about our attitudes towards marine life. "When people talk about 'wildlife,' they're not talking about fish," she claims. "A whale can be wildlife, a seal can be wildlife, but an octopus isn't. People who say they are vegetarians will eat fish." Recreation ads with grinning people holding dead fish drive Lash wild. Try that with a furry animal, she says, and see what happens. She laments the lack of connection we have with underwater creatures—out of sight, out of mind—and feels this absence makes it easier for us to believe we have the right to fish anywhere. Considering how important the ocean is to human life—how everything comes from the sea to start with—Lash considers our backwardness ironic, and foolish.

Ocean yields are declining in B.C.—down 20 percent since 1987. Harvesting techniques are sophisticated and relentless. And we are fishing further and further down the food chain, weakening ecosystems and making recovery more difficult for top-level, fish-eating species. Even fishers are beginning to accept that no-take areas make sense; marine animals must have some sanctuaries in order to revive. Consider B.C.'s commercially valuable rockfish, which have suffered a catastrophic population downturn. Nearly forty species of these colourful reef residents frequent our waters. They settle in one area for life, grow very slowly and can live up to 140 years. A network of protected reefs would help them rebuild their numbers and seed surrounding areas with new inhabitants.

Protected areas are savings plans for depleted fish stocks: in these accounts you allow your capital to grow untouched. They are substitutes for the natural refuges eliminated by our "improved" technologies. Preserving spawning grounds and other delicate marine ecosystems may enable us to help scarce or valued species regenerate themselves. With enough refuges, stocks might sustain themselves or even increase. There are no guarantees: fish migrate; pollution pays scant attention to boundaries. But it's a start.

Lash points to the province's abalone industry as an example of a tragedy that need not have occurred. Abalone reproduce by "broadcasting" eggs and sperm into the water; fertilization is only ensured if concentrations of adult animals are sufficiently high. Because they were harvested indiscriminately for years, abalone concentrations have become so low that the species is virtually sterile. It may never recover. As a result, today there is a total ban on abalone fishing on the B.C. coast. "If we had protected some nursery areas," says Lash, "we might be a lot better off right now."

Twenty-two countries, including New Zealand, Australia and South Africa, have established no-take marine refuges. Even the United States, whose sanctuary program "doesn't really have a lot of teeth to it," according to Lash, is beefing up regulations. The results are beginning to speak for themselves. Twenty-three no-take zones, less than one percent of Florida Keys National Marine Sanctuary, were set aside in 1997; spiny lobster and fish populations are already showing signs of recovery. Studies in South Africa indicate that rockfish densities are five times greater in protected areas than in adjacent waters where the fish are taken. Fish stocks on a Philippines coral reef rebounded after all harvesting was banned on parts of the reef.

Change has been slow in Canada. Parks Canada is drafting legislation to preserve 360 000 hectares of ocean off two national parks: Gwaii Haanas in the Queen Charlottes and Pacific Rim on the west coast of Vancouver Island. The provincial Ministry of Environment, Lands and Parks is working to ensure that a marine component is included in the protected area discussions now taking place on B.C.'s central coast. But saving the sea is more complicated than setting aside land for parks: harvest restrictions must be authorized by the Department of Fisheries and Oceans.

A federal protected area "draft" strategy for the B.C. coast was announced in 1998. It was immediately condemned as inadequate by scientists and conservation groups and still hasn't been approved. "The plan provides minimal protection," says Lash. "A designated area might prohibit kelp harvesting, for instance, but allow fish farming. This strategy will not protect species or promote sustainable fisheries." Forty groups and 150 scientists from sixteen countries joined Living Oceans to urge that a core of no-take zones (not even mentioned in the plan) be established and that marine protected areas have stringent minimum standards: no bottom trawling, finfish aquaculture, dumping, dredging, exploration, development, ballast blowing, introduction of alien species, outfall discharge, artificial reefs or log booming.

Since 1998, the federal government has announced four "pilot" marine protected areas for B.C. Gabriola Passage, where record-sized ling cod once lurked and strong currents help sustain a brilliant landscape of sponges and sea stars, is dear to Lash's heart. She worked for years to preserve this site. Another spot with exceptional diversity is Race Rocks, southwest of Victoria. The final two pilot areas are far offshore. Bowie Seamount, west of the Queen Charlotte Islands, rises over 3000 metres to just below the surface of the ocean; the Endeavour Hot Vents are strange volcanic chimneys on the deep seafloor southwest of Vancouver Island. Both are oases of biological abundance. Indeed, these hot vents and others are home to lifeforms unlike anything scientists have seen before.

The next step with the pilot projects is to identify and implement the form of preservation most suited to each area. This is science in the making, explains Lash. Conservation biologists such as Michael Soulé believe that, for land animals, two things are necessary: core areas with high levels of protection and safe migration routes between core areas. But the design of marine reserves is in its infancy. "One of the reasons we don't have the science," suggests Lash, "is that we don't have any marine protected areas set up to study. We need to learn from them, see whether they should be bigger or smaller, find out which modes of protection work best.

"We also have to make sure that any plan we're working on is adaptable to the science as it becomes available. But at the same time, we can't just do nothing while we're waiting for answers." Thus, we have pilot areas and draft strategies: interim measures. The Living Oceans Society wants to make sure that all interested parties get their say before any decisions are made. Naturally, Lash and her supporters will be arguing for no-take zones. Some who make their living from the ocean will be in agreement. Others, such as sport-fishing and underwater harvesting associations, will likely be opposed. The final result will almost certainly be a compromise.

Regardless, the crusade for the long-term health of the ocean, and the livelihoods of those who depend on it, will continue. A no-take campaign is already in the works for Browning Pass between Nigei and Balaklava islands off northern Vancouver Island. This oceanic canyon, its walls carpeted with colourful invertebrates and home to myriad rockfish, is the proposed site of a major dive resort. Other potential harvest refuges include Khutzeymateen Inlet, Cormorant Channel, Mitlenatch Island, Botanical Beach, Checleset Bay and the Goose Group.

Conservationists promise that fish and their human predators will not be the only species to profit from no-take zones. Marine mammals and plants will benefit as well, of course. And protected areas can play a vital educational role, introducing children to the marvels of the ocean. Recreation opportunities, including whale watching, kayaking and diving, will help the economies of coastal communities. Scientific research and monitoring of no-take zones may result in better managed fisheries. "Marine protected areas aren't the solution to everything," says Lash. "But they are an important thing we have to establish on our coast."

Coastal Villages

At FIRST GLANCE, the British Columbia communities profiled here appear to fall into three neat categories: Kyuquot and Ladner are supported by fishing; Ocean Falls and Telegraph Cove have traditionally relied on forestry; Klemtu and Kincolith are First Nations villages. Together, you'd think, they might portray a representational cross-section of coastal life. But no such luck. They are as different and as varied as half a dozen places can be that share the same coastline.

One thing is certain, however: all are in the grip of change. The forest industry abandoned Ocean Falls and Telegraph Cove years ago. Kyuquot's residents, both First Nation and non-Native, are suffering the effects of a decade-long fisheries downturn. Ladner feels this decline as well, though agriculture has always helped pay the bills there. The six communities are courting—some seriously, some tentatively—the new economic god of tourism.

Most of these settlements are isolated and beyond the reach of a highway, though several have acquired handy new ferry connections. Ladner, in contrast, is practically an urban suburb, yet still off the beaten track. It has almost 20 000 residents. Ocean Falls has 35. I chose these six, large and small, because they have the qualities that count: inspirational settings, friendly inhabitants and little-known but fascinating histories. To me, their vulnerability also makes them appealing. They seem somehow suspended in time, caught between proud, self-sufficient pasts and an unsettled but very human future.

TELEGRAPH COVE

A CURIOUS COASTAL traveller in the first half of this century would soon have noted that many of B.C.'s smaller communities looked much alike. At each port of call, steamship passengers first glimpsed a tight cluster of buildings, usually tucked away in a secluded cove. As the vessel cautiously approached shore, homes, a store, post office, school, Red Cross station, net lofts, boat sheds—and, usually, either a sawmill or a cannery—would come into view, all perched on log pilings and floating docks or connected by boardwalks to a timbered pier. Behind this setting loomed a backdrop of dark evergreens. Everything glistened in the rain.

Nature has reclaimed most of those early hamlets, though their names—Port Essington, Arrandale, Wadhams, Margaret Bay, Georgetown Mills, Kildonan and many others—linger in our history. A few boardwalk villages, including Kyuquot and Namu, still hang on against all odds. Other places, such as the Kitasoo First Nation community of Klemtu, are tearing up their fine wooden walkways and replacing them with concrete and dirt. Timber, once so cheap and plentiful that entire towns were constructed of nothing else, is expensive now and difficult to maintain.

A killer whale skeleton hangs above the entrance to Stubbs Island Whale Watching at Telegraph Cove. (ANDREW SCOTT)

So a first sighting of Telegraph Cove, on northern Vancouver Island about fifty kilometres southeast of Port Hardy, can come as a surprise. The cove is a bit eccentric, perhaps—painstakingly preserved, complete with exhibit-style signs and photographs that explain its history. But it's not a museum piece, like the old gold-rush town of Barkerville. Telegraph Cove is living history: a year-round community with a general store, gift shop, gallery, restaurant and pub, a large marina and a huge campground. It's busiest, of course, in the summer season, when the staff swells to ninety people and visitors come for the kayaking, fishing and whale watching. In winter only a handful of residents remain, and any children ride the bus each weekday to Port McNeill for their schooling, a forty-kilometre round trip.

We show up in late July on our way north to Port Hardy, where we plan to board BC Ferries' mid-coast vessel, the *Queen of Chilliwack,* and go to Bella Bella on the mainland coast. We're just breaking our journey, really, camping overnight and hoping to take a trip out into Johnstone Strait to see some whales. Down at the boat ramp a group of kayakers are getting ready to leave on an expedition. They slowly fit what seems an impossibly large pile of gear and supplies into their tiny craft. Another group, freshly returned from the wilds, celebrates in front of the general store with cones of ice cream, a substance unavailable on the high seas. Thousands of paddlers launch at Telegraph Cove each year in order to explore the network of offshore islands and channels in the Broughton Archipelago and beyond.

The village itself is a study in wood; all the traditional coastal building elements are here in force. We wander the boardwalks and docks, checking out freshly painted cottages cantilevered over the water and stacked up along the steep shoreline. Some are rental units; others serve as employee housing. There's the 1929 Burton House, for instance, built "balloon" style—a cheap construction method that dispensed with internal framing and relied on the roof to hold up the walls. A former floating hospital, which originated further north at the logging camp of O'Brian Bay but fell off its barge while being towed to a new location, is another heirloom. It's hard to tell whether the ancient, rusty truck resting on the pier is an exhibit or a working vehicle.

Several cabins were erected by Japanese employees in the 1930s, then taken away from them in World War II when the country's Japanese Canadians were interned. One such building, now known as Caretaker House, was constructed by Mr. Ogawa, who fabricated boxes for shipping salted salmon. Crouter House, a rebuilt shack moved from the logging railroad terminus of Beaver Cove, is the oldest structure. The most elegant is Wastell House, recently renovated into a hotel and now sporting the decor of the early 1900s.

Telegraph Cove got its name in 1912 when it became home to Bobby Cullerne, a lineman for the new telegraph/telephone line laid that year from Campbell River to northern Vancouver Island. Cullerne lived alone in the cove in a one-room shanty and patrolled the line, which was strung from tree to tree along the shore, in his boat. In the mid-1920s, an uppercrust Englishman named Alfred Marmaduke Wastell, who managed B.C. Packers' box factory at Alert Bay, just across Broughton Strait, built a saltery with Japanese partners on property he owned in the cove. Chum salmon were made ready for markets in Japan and a small sawmill was established.

In the Dirty '30s, after the saltery failed and the fishing company closed down its box factory (it was cheaper to pack tins of salmon in cardboard cartons), Wastell's son, Fred, and Fred's friend and partner, Alex MacDonald, expanded the Telegraph Cove mill. "Rough and finished lumber for all building purposes," its advertising read: "mouldings, doors, windows, firewood." Unfortunately, there was not exactly a roaring demand for specialty lumber at the time. Still, the sawmill managed to stay alive, sustaining a dozen employees and their families through the Depression era.

World War II changed everything. The air force needed lumber to build military bases at Port Hardy, Coal Harbour and Bella Bella, and took all the wood that Telegraph Cove could cut. In the 1930s, desperate men would work for mere room and board. During the war years, it became difficult to find enough employees to man the mill. Eventually, the air force took over the operation, including its tugboat, the *Hili-Kum*. The workforce was increased to sixty-five and a new bunkhouse and huge mess hall constructed. After the war, when the mill was returned to its owners, a mining and forestry boom on northern Vancouver

Island kept the cove's circular saws turning out lumber for bridges and industrial buildings. The mill operated until Fred Wastell's death in 1985, after which it was declared obsolete and shut down.

The amazing current condition of the village is due to the hard work of Gordie and Marilyn Graham, who run Telegraph Cove Resorts and currently own much of the cove's real estate. The Grahams have spent a bundle replacing decayed planks and piles, repairing roofs, modernizing cottage interiors, landscaping, and adding safety railings and such homely touches as window boxes. Their latest venture is the spiffy new Killer Whale Café and Old Saltery Pub, built on the pier and designed to resemble the saltery, now torn down, and blend in with the rest of the historic surroundings.

Gordie Graham logged for years in the Port Alice area, then decided to change careers. "Yup, I'm the guy that hammers the nails here," he says, when I ask him about the maintenance involved in keeping Telegraph Cove spick-and-span. "When we started, it had got really run down. The boardwalk was falling apart and the houses were in terrible condition. But I know about working with saws and big timbers and I love doing this kind of stuff. Over the years you learn all kinds of tricks." Because creosoted lumber was too messy for a public facility, everything was rebuilt with yellow cedar, a rot- and insect-resistant wood that lasts longer than most other types.

Graham and a wood-savvy assistant refurbished the wartime bunkhouse and converted the old mess hall, which had later served as a community hall, dance hall and movie theatre, into accommodation. They turned the original company store and post office at the end of the pier into a gift shop. In front of this building, displayed on a barrel, someone has planted daisies in a pair of exhausted logging boots.

Opposite the gift shop is the headquarters of one of B.C.'s pioneering ecotourism companies, housed in a 1928 freight shed.

Stubbs Island Whale Watching was the first operation of its kind in the province. Above the office entrance, a suspended, six-metre-long skeleton with a fearsome set of white teeth announces the exact species of whale that Stubbs Island's clients are hoping to see. For sixteen years, owner Jim Borrowman has been introducing people to the world of the killer whales, which congregate each year in Johnstone Strait, just outside the cove. There they feast on salmon and rub themselves on the pebble beaches at Robson Bight, sixteen kilometres to the southeast, an ecological reserve that is off-limits to tourists but not, unfortunately, to commercial fishers.

Borrowman takes 10 000 visitors a year on his two tour boats. The eighteen-metre aluminum *Lukwa* holds forty-eight passengers, while the *Gikumi*, an older wooden tug that succeeded the *Hili-Kum* as the workboat at Telegraph Cove and was used to tow logs and haul lumber, can take forty. Besides killer whales, ecotourists might catch a glimpse of Pacific white-sided dolphins, minke and humpback whales— even elephant seals—all of which seem to be increasing in number along the West Coast. We join the *Lukwa* and head out into the middle of Johnstone Strait in calm, sunny weather. Before long, we're surrounded by foraging killer whales.

We're lucky enough to be on hand for a social encounter between several different pods, twenty to twenty-five animals in all. The whales' behaviour becomes quite frisky. The enormous mammals thrust their heads out of the water and look around, a manoeuvre called spy-hopping, and slap their tails and flukes on the surface in seeming excitement. Gisele Landry, who doubles as deckhand and naturalist, throws a hydrophone over the side so we can listen to their squeaks and clicks. A vast Alaska cruiseship on its way south to Vancouver slows to a crawl so a thousand passengers can share the thrill. We hear them whooping as they watch the whales.

Warm sunshine, ocean breezes, show-off cetaceans—this place is paradise, right? Well, not quite. There's a fly in the ointment in the form of a scar on the landscape. We can see the scar from the *Lukwa*. It is the work of Bud Wagner, a Seattle developer. Wagner started coming to Telegraph Cove for vacations and so loved the place, according to Mary Welsh, his development coordinator, that he decided to buy 130 hectares adjacent to the Grahams' resort and transform them into Telegraph Cove Venture, a "planned community." Over a period of eight years, this has involved removing the old sawmill and most of the trees, and then bulldozing the land into a moonscape of rock and gravel to prepare it for dozens of single-family homes and the obligatory golf course. On the bright side, a park and a killer-whale interpretive centre have been promised for the project's shoreline.

In fifty years, or however long it takes for the landscape to regenerate, Telegraph Cove Venture will no doubt look great—and just like every other ritzy planned community on the continent. But right now there's a lot of dust and noise and anger in the air. "I just wish he'd build something," says Gordie Graham. "It's been a friggin' nightmare for us." How ironic. Try to keep a small slice of B.C.'s unique boardwalk-and-floating-dock heritage alive, and what happens? Someone comes along right next door and builds the type of ubiquitous project you can see anywhere in North America. Progress never sleeps.

KINCOLITH

IT'S "BOAT DAY" in Prince Rupert, and the dock that serves outlying north coast communities buzzes with anticipation. Aboard the forty-seat *Centurion IV,* mate Don Gordon is supervising the stowage of boxes of groceries, crated building supplies and dozens of bags. This late-August morning, the boat is almost full with families returning from summer vacation. Rachel and Chris Stanley, for instance, have been to Edmonton and Vancouver with their sons Stuie and Jamaal. "We're dying to get back home," says Rachel. "We can hardly wait to eat our traditional Nisga'a foods again."

The nineteen-metre *Centurion* is the marine lifeline to the historic Nisga'a outpost of Kincolith, or Gingolx, perched on a spectacular bay eighty kilometres north of Prince Rupert near the mouth of the Nass River. For over 130 years, visitors have reached this remotest of B.C. communities by boat or floatplane only. Now a road is snaking its way by fits and starts out of the Nass valley—heartland of the Nisga'a Nation—to connect Kincolith to the world. I want to see the village before its splendid isolation comes to an end.

At 8:30 a.m. sharp, under sapphire skies, we motor out of Prince Rupert harbour and pass the Tsimshian village

Kenny Alexander leads an expedition to search for the gravestones of Kincolith's pioneers at the old Nass Bay cemetery. (ANDREW SCOTT)

of Metlakatla, site of an experimental nineteenth-century settlement by William Duncan, a pioneer Anglican missionary. The *Centurion* has made the twice-weekly journey to Kincolith for fifteen years now. Built in Vancouver in 1980, the privately owned boat first served as the ferry to Lasqueti Island. It's a powerful vessel: twin, 480-horsepower Volvo engines push us through the calm waters of Chatham Sound at nineteen knots—about thirty-five kilometres per hour—throwing up lashings of spray as we head north into Portland Inlet's giant maw.

Passengers spend the three-hour journey chatting or reading. Some sleep; others look out the windows. There's no real promenade deck; for fresh air you must stand astern with the baggage. "Most of the time," says Alex Starr, who has skippered the *Centurion* for its entire history on the north coast, "there's pretty good weather and it's a gorgeous trip. But from October to the end of March, look out. It's nothing to have sixty-knot winds and ten-foot waves. In January and February there's sea fog and freezing spray. There's no point trying to get through then; it's like farting against thunder." Just three trips a year on average are postponed because of weather.

All too soon, the decibel level of the boat's noisy engines declines and we're cozying up to the Kincolith dock. Everyone in the village is here, it seems, and the scene soon becomes one of good-natured chaos. The RCMP are in attendance, as rumour has it that an illegal shipment of alcohol may be arriving. All I see is two constables helping people carry their bags.

Kincolith is a small place, fewer than 400 people. Overlooking the entrance to Nass Bay, it has a fine view down Portland Inlet. To the east and south, 2000-metre-high mountains rise straight out of the ocean. Alaska is just a raven's flight away. Humpbacked salmon are splashing their way up Mission Creek, which borders the village. Herons, bald eagles, crows and seagulls are gathered on the gravel bars.

I settle into a comfortable trailer that Ramona Smythe rents out to visitors, then buy some groceries at the store. Later, as I set out to explore, I'm accompanied by Bingo, a friendly black dog who chases eagles and attaches himself to my heels for the next three days.

Kincolith's history is intriguing. The community was founded in 1867 by a group of Nisga'a led by Philip Latimer and two Anglican Church Missionary Society clergymen, Robert A. Doolan and Robert Tomlinson. Fearing the influence of white traders and alcohol on the main Nisga'a villages further up the Nass River, a band of evacuees built two rafts and floated downstream with their possessions and families. They ended up on Nass Bay, near the site of a short-lived (1831-34) Hudson's Bay post named Fort Nass.

A "model" Christian village, designed after Metlakatla, where everyday life was strictly regulated, soon grew up there. Alcohol and guns were prohibited. Residents had to observe the Sabbath, attend church and send their children to school. By 1870 the population was sixty. Next year, Tomlinson, who had a medical background, opened a three-room hospital, which attracted more settlers. A sawmill provided lumber for houses, school, church and, in later years, for docks, stores, fences and boardwalks. Old photos show a tidy hamlet with the distinct flavour of Victorian England.

In 1884 Reverend William Collison took over. He would stay until his death in 1922. Under his benign influence, which emphasized spiritual matters but left secular leadership to the Nisga'a chiefs and elders, Kincolith became a convenient stopping-place and regional supply centre for river traffic and for the seven salmon canneries that operated in Nass Bay between 1881 and 1942. Kincolith declined in importance along with the cannery trade. By the 1950s, logging roads were closing in on the three upstream Nisga'a villages, linking them to the wider world. Kincolith, meanwhile, was slipping steadily toward its present status of sleepy, exquisite backwater.

An old Anglican church has been the village's dominant structure, joined in prominence since 1989 by a large, red-roofed community centre. While the exterior cladding is not original, the rest of Christ Church, including its interior, dates from 1893, the year a fire destroyed its predecessor (and most of the rest of the village). It is one of the most significant mission structures on the north B.C. coast.

In contrast to other Nisga'a centres, where traditional arts such as dancing, drumming and carving are strongly resurgent, Kincolith is still known as the "holy" village. Harry Moore, band administrator at the time of my visit (also co-chairman of the church committee and superintendent of the Church Army choir), estimates that 75 percent of the inhabitants are Anglican.

There's not much to do in Kincolith. About thirty-five gillnetters and seiners operate out of a little harbour. A salmon enhancement project run by the tribal fisheries agency provides a few jobs, as do construction projects, a logging operation on nearby reserve land, and occasional fishing, hunting and sightseeing charters. The village hopes to start a business that will employ sixty people, producing smoked and frozen salmon. A modern health clinic was built in 1989 at the same time as the community centre, and there's an elementary school (with adult education night classes). The sixty or seventy high school students, however, must move to Prince Rupert or further afield to finish their education.

With Moore's permission, I roam the neatly marked village streets—Percival, Volunteer, Mission, Broad, Fireman, Grassy Point—taking photographs and talking to anyone who will talk back. The serenity and sea air are refreshing, and I wander out to the other dock at the east end of town, used at high tide by floatplanes and small boats. A nineteenth-century cannon, found along with three cannonballs during an extremely low tide in the early 1970s, is mounted there on a rock.

I notice a strange white statue, standing alone in an empty lot with the weeds trimmed all around. I know the cemetery is some distance away, so I'm curious about this marker. The commanding monument is almost life-sized:

a two-headed man with staring eyes, his hands framing a heavy, incised pattern of concentric ovals on his abdomen. Beneath this enigmatic figure is a mysterious inscription:

Here lies the last but not
the least because he is the
last of all His line the
Lak Deyaukl Tribe

| ABEL | Died Ap 25 | SOLOMON |
| WARD | 1911 Age 61 | WARD |

It's not clear whether Abel is the last of his line, or Solomon, or just who exactly is buried here, but there's something compelling about this lone sentinel. It seems to announce the end of a noble heritage, who knows how many centuries old. I feel as if I've run across a harbinger of my own human mortality. Thus it is written, the intense faces seem to say, king or commoner, legend or laughingstock: there is no escape.

Caught up in reverie, I hardly notice the elderly man who has stopped on the road beside me, resting on his stick. He coughs. I look up. I had already greeted this gentleman several times, as he's the only person who seems to walk around as much as I do. "This is where their house was," the old-timer says. "I was living here when Abel died. I was born in 1906 and I'm the oldest person in Kincolith." He flings out an arm. "In the whole valley, I'm the oldest Nisga'a."

This is Rufous Watts, born in Alaska but raised in Kincolith. He left home to work in Ketchikan and Vancouver, then returned when he reached sixty-five and started collecting his pension. That was over twenty years ago. "There were lots of old people in the village when I was a boy," says Watts. "Now there's just one old man. That's me." He explains the village name, Gingol<u>x</u>: *gin*, meaning scalp, and *gol<u>x</u>*, meaning dried. The "place of dried scalps" was an ancient battlefield. One legend has the Nisga'a victorious, one has the Haida; the village name suggests that whoever won seems to have displayed the heads of the losers as a grisly reminder of their power.

Next day I hire Sidney Alexander, a spry septuagenarian who looks ten years younger (I guess Rufous doesn't consider him old), to take me round Nass Bay in his fishing punt. First we head to the cemetery, where his son Kenny guides me through the heavy undergrowth, a rifle slung over his shoulder in case of grizzly contact. We find polished marble gravestones from last century, one surmounted by a mossy carved eagle. "People would come from as far away as Kitkatla and Hartley Bay for an important burial ceremony," says Sidney, "but not any more." Kenny uncovers the final resting place of William Collison, archdeacon of Caledonia, who "devoted 49 years of his life to the uplifting of the native tribes of the north coast, 1873-1922," according to his headstone.

We inspect the old cannery sites that flourished on the Nass: Pacific Northern, Mill Bay, Croasdaile, Nass Harbour, Cascade, Port Nelson, Arrandale. It's amazing how little remains: a few rotten pilings, a rusty boiler. Many Chinese and Japanese workers from these lonely spots are buried in Kincolith cemetery. Nass Bay was also famous for the West Coast's largest oolichan fishery. The edible oil or "grease" extracted from this silvery sprat, used as a sauce, is considered a great delicacy. In ancient days, the Nisga'a managed a far-flung trading empire based on the valuable food.

Next morning, former assistant band manager Alvin Nelson tells me a little about Kincolith's past. "When this place was settled," he says, "many traditional values weren't given as high a priority as they were on the upper Nass." It is the only Nisga'a centre without a totem pole, for instance. A brass band, whose fifty musicians have performed as far away as Prince George, is the major cultural institution. Interest in hereditary customs is increasing, though. A dance troupe has been founded, and performers from all four Nisga'a villages danced together for the first time in 1994.

Nelson tells me that Kincolith has the potential for more tourism, especially sportfishing. Considering the area's beauty and its pristine air and water, this seems like a colossal understatement. According to *Centurion* skipper Alex Starr, a world-class round-trip awaits: Prince Rupert to Kincolith and up the Nass River to Aiyansh by boat, then back to Prince Rupert through Terrace by road. Says Starr, "All they have to do is put in a fuel dock at Kincolith and they're laughing."

"People move away from Kincolith," claims Nelson, "because we can't offer them the economic opportunities they can find elsewhere." But with the completion of the road, presently scheduled for the year 2001, who knows? People may return. They may bring the old ways back with them. Perhaps totem poles will even rise in the village. One thing is certain: when the world intrudes on its 130-year-old slumber, Kincolith will surely change.

OCEAN FALLS

BY THE TIME the *Queen of Chilliwack* reaches the head of Cousins Inlet, 480 kilometres northwest of Vancouver, and pulls up to the dock of the silent community, it's one-thirty in the morning. Unsurprisingly, the only soul around is a BC Ferries employee, who meets the boat and lowers the vehicle ramp. Our kayaks are rolled off on one of the handy wheeled racks that ferry staff use for this purpose, and deposited ashore. We ask the lone attendant where we might pitch a tent. He begins to explain that the community campsite is a mile or so away, up a hill by Link Lake. Then he regards our loaded craft and flings a benevolent arm at the semi-abandoned townsite behind him. "Heck, you can camp anywhere," he says. "We don't mind. Welcome to Ocean Falls."

We choose a flat patch of neatly mown lawn, complete with picnic tables, opposite the ferry dock and right beside the old courthouse, which is also home to a postal outlet, a health clinic and various administrative offices. Over the next few days, we share this piece of turf with a large porcupine, which emerges from the bushes each evening to dine on grass shoots at the same time we prepare our meal. The empty shell of the 370-room Martin Inn, once one of the largest hotels in B.C., looms eerily over our campsite.

The shell of the 370-room Martin Inn, at centre, rivals BC Ferries' *Queen of Chilliwack* in size. (ANDREW SCOTT)

Ocean Falls, it's fair to say, is a mere shadow of its former self. The industrial potential of this location was noted early in the century, and the first power and timber leases granted in 1901. Several changes of ownership occurred before the Bella Coola Development Company finally established a sawmill there in 1909, and a pulp mill and dam in 1912. A year later, the company encountered financial difficulties, and in 1915 a new owner, Pacific Mills Ltd., took control.

Pacific Mills, encouraged by the wartime demand for all kinds of raw materials, doubled power generation at the site by raising the dam and added four new paper and newsprint mills. By the end of World War I, the waters of twenty-nine-kilometre-long Link Lake, which had originally dropped into Cousins Inlet in a scenic cascade, were providing electricity for immense pulp, paper and lumber operations.

A thriving company town grew up around the mills. Large numbers of Chinese, Japanese and East Indian workers were hired because of the labour shortages caused by the war, and many of them remained at Ocean Falls, living in segregated accommodations and worshipping at their own Buddhist and Hindu temples. Despite the fact that the company was landlord as well as employer—and butcher, baker and candlestick-maker, as well—a strong community spirit flourished. The townsfolk organized athletic clubs and entertainment groups, including a band, an orchestra, and a musical and dramatic society. After World War II, private entrepreneurs were invited to take over the department store and gas station, and to start other businesses, and Ocean Falls lost a little of its "company town" flavour. Until the mid-1950s, when the population topped out at about 4000, this remote but feisty community was one of the most important on the mainland coast north of Vancouver.

Today it is one of the least important, and the thirty-five or so individuals who live there full-time prefer it that way. This is not to say they're unsociable. Far from it. We spend much of our brief visit talking to them, beginning at a floating restaurant called the Shack, where Connie Lamb is serving breakfast to Norm Brown, who has brought her a huge bunch of tiger lilies and hydrangeas scavenged from long-neglected gardens.

"I keep everyone around here supplied with flowers," Brown tells us. Formerly from Kaslo, in the Kootenay region, he has lived in this "unknown paradise," as he calls it, for eleven years and wears several hats: campground manager, glass installer, historical society president. All residents have multiple vocations, it seems. The postmistress rents out lodging. The gift-shop owner cuts hair. The tax consultant teaches firearms safety and tutors math and physics. Someone else rents boats, leads ecotours and fishing charters, and does landscaping and massage. Where do they all find the time?

After breakfast, we wander the derelict townsite. A few old homes, crumbling apartments and broken-windowed stores still stand. The rainforest, encouraged by a mild, wet climate, lurks at the edge of town, waiting to invade. Though difficult to imagine now, this unlikely place once throbbed with activity. Many a community might envy the facilities built to lure workers and their families to Ocean Falls and keep them content: a hospital, dental offices, laundry, dance hall, cinema, boys' club, tennis courts, bowling alleys, Legion hall—even a yacht club. Perhaps the best-known amenity of all was the twenty-metre swimming pool, home to the remarkable Ocean Falls Swim Club. This well-coached organization produced such champions as Lenora Fisher, who won a gold medal at the 1955 Pan-American Games, and Ralph Hutton, who brought home silver from the 1968 Olympics.

Today's residents have reclaimed numerous structures from the decay. The 1922 Catholic church, St. Margaret's, underwent a loving renovation; the former hospital became the well-equipped Coast Lodge; an old dormitory was transformed into the Ocean Falls Fishing Lodge. The mill itself is intact, though its machinery was auctioned off in 1986. A handful of BC Hydro employees maintain the power plant, which supplies electricity to Bella Bella, a Heiltsuk First Nation town forty kilometres away. Norm Brown has personally taken on the restoration of the 1917 Company House, where visiting Pacific Mills executives used to stay, as a one-man project. He fondly shows us round his incipient museum, and we meet the latest inhabitants: thousands of tiny brown bats, now lodged snugly in the attic.

The decline of Ocean Falls dates from the 1960s, when aging machinery and high transportation costs made it difficult for Crown Zellerbach, the company that owned

Pacific Mills, to compete in world markets. Crown Zellerbach began scaling back its activities. First to go were the sawmill, groundwood mill, one paper machine and 110 workers. Then came a fateful announcement: the entire operation would shut down in 1973. As the closure date drew near, the New Democratic (NDP) provincial government of the day announced an eleventh-hour reprieve for the community, by that time down to 600 inhabitants. The entire townsite was acquired for $800 000 and turned into a Crown corporation.

The purchase slowed the decline of Ocean Falls but failed to halt it. The mill closed for good in 1980, abandoning a five-year contract to supply the *Los Angeles Times* with 30 000 tonnes of newsprint annually. The last few employees dismantled everything of value in town that could be taken away, and most of the townsfolk moved on to new lives elsewhere. A few people decided to stay. Some of them bought homes in Martin Valley, a residential subdivision that had been built in the 1950s on the shores of Cousins Inlet, about two kilometres west of the mill.

Named after Archie Martin, the mill's general manager in the early days, Martin Valley had once been the site of a company farm that supplied fresh eggs, milk and meat to the workforce. In the mid-1980s, after the closing of the plant, perfectly adequate homes could be bought there for about $4000. For less than $50 000 (half that for a fixer-upper), you can still purchase a house in the valley, and many people have taken advantage of this bargain.

We've been offered a camping spot in the backyard of one such house. Its absentee owners are Frank and Shannon Dwyer, the lighthouse keepers at Dryad Point, just north of Bella Bella. We'd met them a few days earlier as we paddled past their century-old station, one of the first lighthouses on the B.C. coast. Frank invited us ashore for coffee, and we spent an agreeable hour talking with the Dwyers. The old-est of their three young children, Carrie and Connor, gave us a tour of the station's equipment, showed us the rose arbour and gardens, and let us refill depleted containers with fresh water.

Our attempt to walk to Martin Valley is thwarted by an ancient truck, whose driver insists we hop aboard for the short ride. He wants to tell us about Ocean Falls. "A third of the folks here are retired and living off fixed incomes," he explains. "Another third are like myself: summer trash, mostly boaters from the United States, who have bought homes here. The final third are just plain weird. A lot of peo-ple here are on welfare. And there's altogether too much drinking in this town."

En route we pass the neighbourhood pub, Saggo's Saloon, which draws a disapproving glance from our chauffeur. On the other side of the road is the cemetery. We get out at the Rain Country Store, an establishment named for the fact that Ocean Falls gets 170 centimetres of the wet stuff every year. A wide concrete ramp enters the ocean nearby. As we admire the seaplanes lined up on the ramp's apron, a veter-an Grumman Goose amphibian aircraft, operated by Pacific Coastal Airlines, lands in the inlet, laboriously wheels itself up onto the apron and spits out a single passenger.

We search the unsigned streets for the Dwyer property and meet more inhabitants. Joe, from Edmonton, is a long-time summer visitor and home owner who has recently decided to live year-round in Ocean Falls. Oliver, a retired high-school teacher from Burnaby, has been a full-time resi-dent now for several years. Everyone, it seems, has plenty of time to chat. "I love meeting people and talking to them," exclaims Oliver. "Sometimes I get into trouble with my wife when I'm supposed to be out doing chores and instead I spend a couple of hours yakking to someone." We find the house we're looking for but decide it's too much trouble to change campsites. We like it fine where we are.

Back in town, Norm Brown tells us that the population of Ocean Falls triples in summer as the part-timers arrive to enjoy the fishing and the quiet. Every six days (less frequently in winter), the *Queen of Chilliwack* makes an afternoon appearance in the inlet. "That's when the town's population doubles again," says Brown. As the vessel glides into view, he rides his bicycle down to the dock, bringing with him a handsome bouquet of flowers for the ferry staff. Someone sets up a booth to sell ice cream and copies of *Rain People*, a history of the town. Gwen Swan, who was born in Ocean Falls and left in 1980 but now returns every summer, sets out two enormous scrapbooks for tourists to leaf through.

Tens of thousands of people passed through this community in its glory days. Ocean Falls was big enough, and had sufficient urban drawing power, that everywhere on the central and northern B.C. coasts one can find individuals who have, at one time or another, worked or lived or visited there—or whose parents or grandparents did so. Often, Swan explains, the ferry passengers are ex-residents or their descendants who have come to revisit scenes of joy and sorrow.

Every few years a spirited reunion is held. Swan, of course, brings along her scrapbooks and encourages participants to pencil in a few more names beside the faces in the photographs. It appears that many former inhabitants of Ocean Falls cannot completely eradicate the place from their systems. They keep coming back for one last, longing glimpse at this village of lost but contented souls that clings to the edge of the world.

KYUQUOT

THE SMOOTH WATERS just ahead of the kayak ripple in expectation and a sleek, bewhiskered head pops up from below. It's a sea otter. The creature rests on its back, clutching a spiny purple sea urchin to the cream-coloured fur of its chest, and gazes at me solemnly. Once hunted to near extinction for their fine, thick coats, sea otters are making a comeback in British Columbia. A few dozen animals transplanted in the early 1970s from Alaska to the Bunsby Islands, just to the north of me, have spread out along northern Vancouver Island's wild outer coast and now number in the hundreds.

I'm probably not the first kayaker this otter has seen, but I'm treated with caution nonetheless. Kayakers get similar looks at nearby Kyuquot, a village of 300 souls, many of whom are dubious about the benefits of tourism and fear the loss of their traditional way of life. Half Scandinavian fishing community, half Nuu-chah-nulth First Nation reserve, Kyuquot is spread over several islands at the mouth of Kyuquot Sound, some 145 kilometres northwest of Tofino. It is one of few safe anchorages in this part of the world, and I'm spending a week there in September, using the outpost as a base for exploring this secluded area.

Houpsitas, a Nuu-chah-nulth First Nation village on Vancouver Island, is part of the community of Kyuquot. (ANDREW SCOTT)

You cannot get to Kyuquot by car. It's either an expensive floatplane ride, which seems like cheating, or else you come by boat, which is not so easy. Larger vessels must run a treacherous gauntlet of exposed and often fogbound coast, studded with rocks and shoals. Small ones have to be hauled over rough logging roads from the Island Highway to upper Kyuquot Sound, then piloted west. I arrive on the *Uchuck III*, a fifty-two-year-old former minesweeper, now one of B.C.'s last old-time coastal freighters, which makes the ten-hour voyage from Muchalat Inlet to Kyuquot weekly, supplying the community with most of its needs.

At the end of the government wharf is the general store. Above it are inexpensive rooms with shared bathroom, kitchen, laundry and living area, complete with wood-burning stove. I've arranged to stay there when not paddling. Sam Kayra, who grew up in Kyuquot and whose pioneer Finnish parents ran the store and helped found an early B.C. fishing association, shows me where to park my gear. Then she ferries visitors over by boat to a tiny restaurant on the reserve where the dinner choices are grilled halibut and roast venison, both delicious and as fresh as they come.

Crows wake me early next morning by dropping shells on the roof. The *Uchuck* is leaving. I wave goodbye from the sundeck of my temporary abode, cantilevered over the water with a fine view of all community comings and goings. Weather permitting, the boat will be back next week. But what do I care? My kayak is tied to the dock. I have a bag full of books. Let it rain and blow. I'll be happy to stay here all winter if necessary.

Exploring Walters Island, the heart of Kyuquot, doesn't take long. Narrow trails twist through a never-logged forest of thousand-year-old spruce and cedar trees; one leads to a beach facing Nicolaye Channel and a cluster of islands where a lighthouse blinks its warning. Beyond them it's a straight run to Russia. On the opposite side of Walters, a few dozen homes—some built with bits and pieces taken from abandoned canneries, some empty and derelict—are connected by boardwalks. There's a small fish-packing plant, a marine gas station, a community hall, no cars. Tentacles of floating dock snake out into Walters Cove. "Thirty-five years ago," *Uchuck* skipper Fred Mather had told me earlier, "most coastal communities looked like this."

Next day, I break out the kayak for a nose around. A Red Cross station and a fishing lodge each occupy their own private chunks of rock; a dozen homes are strewn over several other isles. Small boats whiz back and forth. Kyuquot is a simple place. You pump your own well water and do without electricity after ten p.m., when generators shut down. If you meet someone on the trail or the water, you stop for a chat.

And you keep an eye open for Miss Charlie, a tame and aging seal who scrounges handouts by the dock.

Paddling a few hundred metres to Vancouver Island, where the elementary school and church are located, I pay a courtesy visit to the Kyuquot band office and ask manager Martha Tyerman about visiting the outlying islands that are part of the tribal reserve. "We don't have a problem with that," she tells me. I must, however, stay away from two small islets that used to serve as the band's ancestral burial grounds.

Later, under clear, calm skies, I cross Nicolaye Channel and glide into Barter Cove, where American sailing ships anchored two centuries ago and traded muskets and metal implements for the lustrous sea otter pelts that would make their owners' fortunes. On Aktis Island, just ahead, half a dozen buildings are all that's left of a once flourishing Native village with a population of 800. No trace is left of the Roman Catholic mission that once perched on Kamils Island to my left. Today, the forest grows where totems used to stand. Bald eagles patrol silent beaches.

The Kyuquot and Checleset tribes (part of the larger Nuu-chah-nulth First Nation) were the region's original residents. In their winter villages, each extended family occupied a cedar-sided longhouse decorated with carved ceremonial figures. They lived well from the rich bounty of land and water, using large dugout canoes for fishing, whaling and defence. The Kyuquots controlled the trade in rare dentalia shells. This slender white mollusc was laboriously plucked from its underwater home with an ingenious "broom" of yew quills that was poked into the sand at the end of a twenty-metre handle. Shaped like miniature elephant tusks, the ten-centimetre-long dentalia were strung in lengths and worn as symbols of wealth and status by Native people all over North America.

In the late nineteenth century, many Kyuquots and Checlesets moved to a former summer village on Aktis Island, which became the regional trading centre. After the sea otters were gone, people sold dogfish oil, went fur sealing in Alaska and worked at the nearby whaling station of Cachalot, which was later turned into a pilchard processing plant. Soon the seals and whales and pilchards were gone, too, and residents caught salmon for a living. Today, even that traditional B.C. industry is in trouble.

The non-Native community on Walters Island got its start in the early years of this century. When Cachalot ran out of prey, many Norwegian whalers settled at Kyuquot and went fishing instead. Other Scandinavians joined them from elsewhere in Kyuquot Sound and from Winter Harbour in Quatsino Sound further north. A boatways and a sawmill were established, and a trollers' cooperative formed that eventually expanded to become one of the most influential fishing organizations in the province.

Today, with the industry in decline, ecotourism is on many people's lips. Elemental and unspoiled, this tempestuous stretch of coast has an undeniable attraction for adventurers. My days are spent scouting windswept rocks and reefs round dozens of local islands. The air is filled with salt and spray and the cries of seabirds. The water is so clear I can look over the side—a popular way to capsize, this—and watch fish swim between leafy strands of giant kelp ten metres below the surface. Tidal pools are marine flower gardens of bright anemones and sea stars. Crabs march through fields of undulating, blue-green eelgrass.

I meet dozens of kayakers, many of them travelling north to the singular wilderness of Brooks Peninsula, a vast promontory off Vancouver Island that the last ice age managed to miss. One sunny morning, two newfound companions and I head to Spring Island, a paradise of gnarled trees and driftwood where an angry ocean has carved arches and stacks out of rock. We search white sand beaches for glass fishnet floats and hike to a former radar base on a grassy bluff. Today only a concrete foundation and a few wires indicate that twenty people once lived at this lonely, exhilarating spot.

Kyuquot tolerates but does not embrace my visit. "We just don't have the facilities to handle many visitors," Sam Kayra explains. Kayakers, who are hardy and self-propelled, and don't usually pollute or make excessive noise or deplete the area's resources (though they sometimes go where they're not supposed to), are slowly gaining community acceptance. Sportfishers, however, have a reputation for not always treating the area with respect. "This summer we had people camping on our favourite beach," she says, "people pulling up water and phone lines with their anchors."

"Kyuquot is about as close to a working model of anarchy as you can get," says Tom Pater, the regional district's elected representative. Some village residents, he acknowledges, fear tourism will put property prices out of their reach. Pater is more concerned with getting Kyuquot a decent water supply and maybe a BC Hydro hookup. Kayra's not even sure she wants to be plugging into the power grid. "What else would that bring?" she wonders. "We sure don't want a road."

The week soon passes. Before I know it, the *Uchuck* is back. As I contemplate the long journey home, I consider Kayra's fears. For now, I think, isolation and infamous weather should protect Kyuquot from the tourist hordes. But in the long term, even this far-flung settlement may not be safe from the outside world.

LADNER

LIKE MANY SMALL TOWNS, Ladner has a memorial to its founder. The monument stands on the main street, near the gaudy, painted totem poles in front of the old municipal hall and next to Uncle Herbert's Fish & Chips. It is plain and sturdy—a cairn of granite blocks with a clock at the top—and it suits the civic spirit. I lived in this community for six years, and as I made my rounds, I'd often pause at William Henry Ladner's shrine and reflect. What would this first settler think today of the town named after him? Would he be spinning in his grave at the inevitable changes, or resting peacefully, content with his creation?

I enjoyed rambling around Ladner in the evening, with small-town sounds drifting by on the breeze. Mangled clarinet squawks escaped from the second-floor windows of the Delta Community Music School. Fishers called out to each other as they spread and mended their nets beside the harbour. Late-working farmers trundled down the street with tractor-loads of potatoes. In summer, mellow sunshine poured over the scene like corn syrup. I could imagine I'd been transported into a fictional landscape—something by Garrison Keillor, perhaps. Certainly, it was easy to forget we were only a thirty-minute drive south of downtown Vancouver.

A troller is moored beside a nineteenth-century warehouse at Ladner's historic fishing harbour. (ANDREW SCOTT)

Forgetting Vancouver, where I'd lived before, was okay with me in those days. Still is, for that matter. The city has grown too crowded and noisy for my liking. But I needed to be close to it for work and friends and family. As a compromise, I moved to this fishing and agricultural centre of about 20 000 people in the municipality of Delta, near the mouth of the Fraser River. It was a fine place to live.

More than any other community in the Lower Mainland, Ladner has kept a village atmosphere. In consequence, so many movies and TV shows have been shot there that some residents find the film crews and their enormous vehicles a nuisance. With dozens of well-kept Victorian and Edwardian buildings, the downtown core has genuine charm, while the outskirts are rife with parks and places to walk, bike, boat, ride horses and see wildlife. You can visit a llama farm, buy salmon off the dock or dine at an outstanding French restaurant. As a bonus, Delta municipality gets more sun and less rain than anywhere else in the Vancouver region.

William Ladner and his younger brother Thomas were two determined Cornishmen who immigrated first to Wisconsin, then travelled by covered wagon to the Pacific coast and finally found their way to British Columbia during the gold rush of 1858. They worked at mining, prospecting and logging, then invested their earnings in a mule packtrain and a general store. William and Thomas married sisters from Victoria, Mary and Edney Booth, and began diking and draining land in the lower Fraser delta in the late 1860s. The families were soon engaged in some of the first serious farming to take place in the Fraser Valley. William moved onto his farm in 1868, Thomas two years later.

In the early years, most of the work was done by hand. To get at the best alluvial soil, impenetrable thickets of hardhack had to be cleared. All dikes and ditches were dug manually. There were no roads. Families were large in those days, and houses lacked insulation, appliances or conveniences. The Ladner brothers, without any machinery more sophisticated than simple ox-drawn ploughs and harrows, grew wheat, oats and hay, and raised cattle and other goods for sale to Victoria, Nanaimo and New Westminster.

During the 1870s and '80s, more settlers arrived in the area and began working the rich alluvial soil. The farmers cooperated with one another, and the appearance of more modern equipment, such as threshers and balers, made the work slightly easier. The riches of the Fraser were also gleaned. Seventeen canneries eventually lined Delta's shores, harvesting the abundant salmon runs. (Only a few old pilings remain.) By the late 1800s, a village had formed, called Ladner's Landing. It became a riverboat stop, and agricultural produce was sent to Vancouver and New Westminster. Many residences date from these early days, especially along 48 and 47A avenues, and avid wanderers will discover other old homes scattered around the townsite.

Ladner's central core retains the vestiges of an entire heritage townscape. Highrises are forbidden in this zone. New construction must blend in. Many old buildings have been lost over the years, of course, but many remain: three quaint churches; the 1912 Tudor-style municipal hall, now a museum; a beautiful 1895 waterfront warehouse; a Masonic lodge handsomely refurbished as lawyers' offices; an ancient livery stable; and several turn-of-the-century storefronts, net lofts and sheds. Residents have even imported old houses from elsewhere. In 1992, Frank Lipton, a custom furniture-maker, barged a dilapidated 1908 Richmond schoolhouse to the town centre and completely restored it for use as a workshop.

Agriculture continues to be Ladner's lifeblood, and the community is surrounded south, east and west by fields of corn, cabbages, beans, peas, potatoes, strawberries, blue-berries, cranberries and other produce. "Respect Slow-Moving Farm Traffic," say signs leading into town. In summer, city slickers become berry pickers as they swarm to the U-pick locations. And if you live in Ladner, you don't have to stop growing things just because you're old. The seniors centre, a lovely 1895 converted farmer's home called McKee House, sports the best-looking vegetable garden out back I've ever seen.

While the Fraser River is no longer essential for trans-portation, and the canneries are long gone, Ladner still sup-ports a sizeable fleet of gillnetters and seiners and several seafood-processing plants. Marinas and a yacht club serve a thirsty crowd of recreational boaters and fishers. Many of

Canada's top rowers practise in nearby Deas Slough, where they glide over the unruffled lagoon like water-spiders in their tiny, eggshell-thin sculls.

In some ways, the river defines the town; wherever the two meet, substantial dikes are meticulously maintained to protect the flat, low-lying land from floods. The dikes also provide some of the best walking and bicycling in B.C., with panoramic marine and rural views and the opportunity to see muskrats, rabbits, coyotes, seals, hawks, snowy owls and huge flocks of sandpipers and other shorebirds.

Directly offshore is a maze of wetlands, the South Arm marshes, part of the great estuary of the Fraser. When I lived in Ladner, I spent much time exploring this rare expanse of natural habitat from the vantage point of a kayak. It's a dynamic place, a bird-rich landscape of shifting sloughs and mudflats, grasses and rushes. The scenery, lush and compelling, is somehow un-Canadian. It has a tropical feel, jungly and swamplike, pungent with decay—a west-coast Everglades. You half expect a crocodile to launch itself off a silty bank or a python to drop from a branch.

Paddling through these muddy channels, I sometimes sensed I was inside a gigantic organ—nature's equivalent of a heart or a lung—endlessly pumping the river's thick, organic liquids in and out of the estuary. The dark tidal waters pulsed over the mucous membrane of the marsh, fertilizing it with a biotic litter until it bloomed with life of its own. At night, especially, the strange beauty of the delta could be visceral. It was hard to shake the feeling that one careless move might get you devoured. One evening, for instance, kayaking alone, I startled a harbour seal, which made a panicky splash that almost tipped my craft. I don't know who was more frightened, me or the seal. I thought I'd disturbed some great swamp monster.

Amazingly, the South Arm marshes didn't even exist a hundred years ago. Ladner's main wharf, now hidden away at the end of a muddy cul-de-sac that is gradually silting up, used to jut directly into the main channel of the Fraser. Decades of farmland diking—plus a long training wall built in the 1920s and '30s to direct the flow of the river and create a safe shipping route—have completely changed the hydrology of the lower Fraser. Broad tidal flats built up behind the training wall in what was once a wide, mostly open reach of river between the municipalities of Richmond and Delta.

At first, the mudflats were colonized by spikerush, bulrush and water horsetail, then by sedge, creeping bentgrass, arrowhead and other plants. As they grew higher, new species emerged: tall fescue, tufted hairgrass, aster, water plantain and checker mallow. Eventually, the dominant plant of the high marsh—the cattail—appeared. An introduced species, purple loosestrife, is now threatening to displace native plants. Scientists are trying to control it with a non-native beetle, which feeds on the colourful invader.

In time, the flats reached island size and height. Above high tide, willow, red osier, alder and cottonwood trees grew. Despite the realtor's oft-heard claim that it isn't being made any more, over 600 hectares of new land were created in little more than a human lifetime. Some of the delta's larger islands, which had been present in vestigial form before the settlers arrived, were also diked and farmed. The owner of Kirkland Island, for instance, raised dairy cattle and shipped milk to the mainland for sale. Later, wealthy Vancouverites— including H.R. MacMillan, the forest-industry baron, and William Farrell, first president of BC TEL (now Telus)— used several islands as private shooting clubs. Today, they are preserved as wildlife habitat.

You can look out at the islands from the mainland dike west of Ladner. As you walk along, you'll pass a condominium complex that stands where B.C.'s third-largest Chinatown used to flourish. Before burning down in 1929, it comprised a dozen businesses and 350 inhabitants, most of whom worked in the canneries or as dike builders. Further on, a marvellous collection of waterfront and floating homes begins. Some are motley and decaying into the foreshore; others are quite distinguished. A painter and a glassmaker have studios there, and a delightful bed and breakfast operates.

If you continue walking, you soon come to neighbouring Port Guichon, where French farmer Laurent Guichon built a hotel and dock in the 1880s and a number of Croatian fishermen later settled. In 1903, a railway line from central Surrey ended there, and connected with a regular trainferry to Victoria. Many of Guichon's descendants still live in the area, and the 1891 Guichon family home has been artfully restored. Further west along the dike, just beyond the bridge to Westham Island, is Canoe Pass, B.C.'s largest floathome community, where all houses must meet strict environmental and design criteria.

At the northern end of Westham Island is the area's biggest tourist attraction: the George C. Reifel Migratory Bird Sanctuary. The estuary of the Fraser River is a vital staging area and nursery for juvenile salmon and home to more bird species—at least 230—than any other B.C. location. Reifel's fertile marshes and mud banks attract a million and a half migratory birds annually. Blinds allow human visitors to view hawks, eagles, owls, geese and many different kinds of ducks and wading birds. Serious birders may spot a rare species, such as a gyrfalcon or a black-crowned night heron. A pair of sandhill cranes often lurks round the entrance. In early November each year, more than 20 000 snow geese descend on Reifel and Westham Island.

Development, of course, is the shadow that looms over all pretty backwaters like Ladner. Residents can only hope their community's rate of growth will be gradual. So far, so good. William Henry Ladner, I feel, would be pleased. You can still wander deep into Ladner Marsh and hear the red-winged blackbirds trill their joyful melodies. You can play eight-ball at Heritage Cue, the ninety-year-old pool hall. The carol ships continue to come to the harbour in winter. Every night, the bald eagles roost down Ferry Road (I once counted fifty of them), where a car-ferry used to cross the Fraser before the George Massey Tunnel was built. And there are other secret places, which I'm keeping to myself.

I believe William Henry would have wanted it that way.

KLEMTU

MIDNIGHT HAD LONG GONE, but the young Kitasoo dancers still chanted and whirled, their red-and-black button blankets flashing images of killer whale, raven, eagle and wolf at a transfixed audience. They had more energy than we did, and eventually Katherine and I slipped out of the school gymnasium into the dark. The sky was washed in starlight, and we walked down the hill to the water where a fine wooden boardwalk stretched from one end of this isolated First Nations village to the other.

The dancers were twirling because the day had been a memorable one. It had been the first day, in fact, in nineteen years that a passenger vessel had made a scheduled stop at Klemtu, 220 kilometres north of Port Hardy—and the first day in history that a villager could drive away from his Swindle Island home on a regular vehicle ferry. Earlier, under sunny skies, with a stream of bright flags snapping in the breeze, BC Ferries' refurbished *Queen of Chilliwack* had cruised from Bella Bella, up Seaforth Channel and across Milbanke Sound into Finlayson Channel, then squeezed through a narrow passage into Klemtu's beautiful little cove.

This happened in 1996, and I was fortunate to have been there. We were spending a week on the central coast to

Heiltsuk First Nation chiefs from Klemtu and Bella Bella gather to greet the inaugural visit of BC Ferries' *Queen of Chilliwack.* (ANDREW SCOTT)

write newspaper and magazine articles about the new ferry service from Port Hardy to Bella Coola, but it was pure luck that we found ourselves on this inaugural voyage to Klemtu. Ferry corporation officials and dignitaries had joined the *Queen* at Shearwater on Denny Island, next door to Bella Bella. Forty Heiltsuk musicians and dancers were aboard as well, in full traditional regalia, plus an assortment of tourists.

As we left Milbanke Sound and entered Finlayson Channel, the landscape changed, from mostly horizontal to mostly vertical. Here was fjordland with a vengeance. Glacier-carved mountains rose out of the sea to heights of 800 metres, while beneath us, the ocean-filled valley dropped away to alarming depths. The ship cruised over the deepest recorded spot on the entire B.C. continental shelf: 418 fathoms, or over 764 metres. Ahead of us, the symmetrical silhouette of Cone Island, known locally as China Hat, marked the entrance to Klemtu Passage. In this protected waterway, two men paddling a handsome dugout canoe appeared and began to pace the slowly moving ferry. Then a powerful Coast Guard inflatable joined the dugout. Soon a flotilla of small craft had gathered round the ship to escort us to the dock.

Klemtu put on a royal welcome for its visitors. The entire village of 400 people, including a row of dignified chiefs in ermine-and-abalone headdresses, showed up to meet the *Queen*. The Heiltsuk dancers chanted and drummed as the passengers disembarked and the vehicles were driven off. The senior chiefs—Archie Robinson and Percy Starr of Klemtu, Edwin Newman of Bella Bella and Frank Rhodes of BC Ferries—made speeches of greeting and congratulation. Carved and painted paddles and other gifts were exchanged. Then everyone fell on a massive feast, including baked salmon, bannock and deep-fried geoduck clams. The celebrations had the feel of another era—of a time when steamship visits were keenly anticipated and provided a crucial link between B.C. coastal communities and the rest of the world.

Klemtu had worked hard over the preceding months in order to furnish its anticipated influx of visitors with places to stay and things to do. Tent and recreational vehicle sites had been built (though there was really nowhere on Swindle Island to drive to). Several bed-and-breakfast operations were open, as was the two-suite Swindle Inn. Fishing and boating charters were available. "People are surprisingly willing and open to making tourism work," explained Chanelle Robertson, Klemtu's tourism consultant, who had been training a group of shy but enthusiastic young villagers as guides. Curious travellers will be able to take a tour of Klemtu, enjoy a traditional meal, watch a dance performance and learn about the community's unusual history.

Klemtu is unique from a linguistic perspective. Its inhabitants descend from two First Nations groups that speak completely different languages. The Kitasoo are the southern-most Tsimshian-speaking tribe; their traditional territories include Laredo Sound and parts of Princess Royal Island, north of Klemtu. The XaiXais are the northernmost branch of the Heiltsuk First Nation, whose language is part of a linguistic family known as Wakashan. They once lived to the east of Finlayson Channel and had village sites at Poison Cove and Kynoch Inlet. By about 1875, the population of both groups had declined so precipitously that many people decided to join together and establish a new settlement nearer the main shipping routes. They earned money cutting cordwood for coastal steamers, and Klemtu became a refuelling stop.

By the 1890s, a white trader had taken up residence and a church had been built. The population of China Hat, as the village was called then, was about fifty. Christianity made slower inroads here than it did at many other coastal locations. Missions were established from time to time, and converts made, but for the most part Klemtu resisted the efforts of those who would baptize its inhabitants and remained true to traditional customs.

The word Klemtu, which was adopted in 1902 as the official village name, may derive from a Tsimshian term meaning "to anchor" or "to tie something." Then again, it may mean "hidden passage." (The origin of Swindle Island's name, which sounds intriguing, has unfortunately been lost.) A safe or hidden anchorage, certainly, is one of Klemtu's most valuable features. A small salmon saltery was built on the cove at the turn of the century, and in 1927 J.H. Todd and Sons estab-lished a substantial cannery there, which provided employ-ment for villagers and other workers until 1968.

After the cannery shut down, an adequate livelihood became more of a struggle for residents. A salmon hatchery and an experimental aquaculture operation provided a few extra jobs, but most villagers rely on commercial fishing to survive.

Stewart Marshall's watercolour paintings show the B.C. coast in its wildest and most inaccessible moods. (ANDREW SCOTT)

Two adult male killer whales and a juvenile cruise down Johnstone Strait. (ALEXANDRA MORTON)

This Pender Island design by Mark Osburn and Wayne Clarke features retracting walls that open to the elements. (Courtesy Osburn/Clarke Productions)

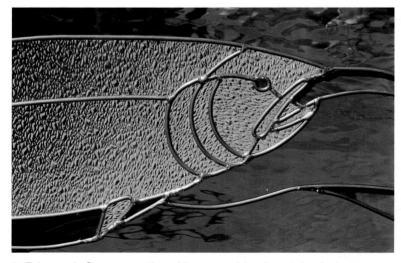

At Telegraph Cove on northern Vancouver Island, a stained-glass salmon spruces up the entrance to the Killer Whale Café. (Andrew Scott)

Peter Schmidt demonstrates the scale of the wood sculptures he is crafting for the Surrey Memorial Hospital.
(ANDREW SCOTT)

An old truck reaches the end of the road at the Telegraph Cove wharf.
(ANDREW SCOTT)

The remote Nisga'a village of Kincolith is hidden away on the shores of Nass Bay on B.C.'s north coast. (ANDREW SCOTT)

Both dogs and fishing boats are serene at Waglisla, the Heiltsuk First Nation community on Campbell Island. (ANDREW SCOTT)

Despite the decrepit appearance of these waterfront cottages, the Walters Cove community at Kyuquot is very much alive. (ANDREW SCOTT)

A decorative dugout canoe marks the shoreline at Klemtu, a Kitasoo village perched on a picturesque Swindle Island cove. (Andrew Scott)

You can get the best breakfast in town at the Shack, Connie Lamb's floating restaurant in Ocean Falls. (Andrew Scott)

A B.C. coastal icon, the arbutus can reach a height of forty metres and a trunk girth of over five metres. (ANDREW SCOTT)

On an islet overlooking Welcome Passage on the Sunshine Coast, a cluster of chocolate lilies nod in the spring breeze. (ANDREW SCOTT)

The great blue heron and the bald eagle may be engaged in a territorial tug of war on the B.C. coast. (Ross Vennesland)

The ancient murrelet is named for the white head feathers that supposedly make it look old. (Courtesy Laskeek Bay Conservation Society)

BC Ferries' smallest vessel, the *Dogwood Princess II* serves Gambier and Keats islands in Howe Sound. (ANDREW SCOTT)

Skun'gwaii (Ninstints) in the southern Queen Charlotte Islands preserves the last extant collection of Haida totem poles. (ANDREW SCOTT)

These portable egg incubators allow salmon enhancement efforts to be applied to the smallest stream. (COURTESY WORLD FISHERIES TRUST)

The *Nanaimo Tillicum,* built in 1924, enjoys a much-deserved retirement as Captain Bill Thompson's pleasure craft. (ANDREW SCOTT)

Traces of former grandeur: the remains of a Kwakwaka'wakw longhouse at Mamalilaculla on Village Island. (ANDREW SCOTT)

The tiny community of Echo Bay on Gilford Island serves a throng of U.S. and Canadian pleasure boaters in summer. (ANDREW SCOTT)

Oops! The winch has jammed. Just kidding. An expectant paddler is "wet launched" from the *Uchuck III* in Tahsis Inlet. (ANDREW SCOTT)

Frank Brown takes a breather from his ecotourism business at McLoughlin Bay (Bella Bella) on Campbell Island. (ANDREW SCOTT)

Murray Mitchell prepares a salmon barbecue for hungry kayakers at Harwood Island, a Sliammon First Nation reserve. (ANDREW SCOTT)

The author enjoys a relaxing paddle in fine weather en route to Flores Island in Clayoquot Sound. (KATHERINE JOHNSTON)

A campsite for one: the mountains of Vancouver Island frame Clayoquot Sound from this tiny Vargas Island beach. (KATHERINE JOHNSTON)

Princess Margaret Provincial Marine Park on Portland Island has dozens of coves perfect for exploring by kayak. (Andrew Scott)

The old Foote farmhouse has sat beside Home Bay on Jedediah Island since the early 1900s. Its future is uncertain. (Andrew Scott)

The lighthouse keepers of Merry Island have been watching over the Strait of Georgia for ninety-seven years. (ANDREW SCOTT)

Today, Klemtu boasts a Transport Canada wharf, a well-equipped general store, a café, a modern fuel facility, a health clinic and an elementary school. The community operates its own hydroelectric plant, the dream of Chief Percy Starr, who managed to persuade government officials to help the village replace its noisy, expensive diesel generator. One thing you won't find, however, is a liquor outlet: Klemtu is "dry" by choice.

After the death of its only industry and the cessation of steamship service, Klemtu became an almost-forgotten backwater. The community's pleasure at being reconnected to the rest of the province by ferry was so obvious in 1996, and its inhabitants so friendly and welcoming, that we manage to find our way back to the village a couple of years later. Tourism hasn't exactly transformed Klemtu, we discover. A few improvements have been made to the dock, but the place looks much the same as it did before. The cove is still pristine and beautiful, the surrounding forests intact, the villagers as outgoing as ever. To our delight, the boardwalk, one of the longest and finest in British Columbia, has not yet been replaced by concrete and pavement, as it's slated to be.

Wooden boardwalks were once a hallmark of coastal communities. When it was built, in the mid-1960s, Klemtu's was the longest in North America. At first, the federal Indian Affairs department refused to fund its construction, but after much persuasion it gave the village $150 000 for materials, and the villagers donated their labour. There were no vehicles in Klemtu at the time, and the boardwalk was designed for pedestrians, baby strollers and bicycles only. Later, "step-asides" had to be cut for pickup trucks, which can just squeeze their way along the structure. Some step-asides are equipped with benches, and boardwalk conversations are frequent. It can take quite a while to get from one end of the walk to the other. Now, with ferry access, the automobile is king and the walkway an inconvenient anachronism. Sadly, its days are numbered.

Down on the dock we see that the *Lillian D* is in town. This vessel, built in 1926 for the B.C. Forest Service, is a floating store and has been visiting remote First Nations communities such as Klemtu, Kitkatla and Hartley Bay for thirty summers. Its present owners, Barry and Rose, live aboard with their two children and spend three or four days at a time at each village. As we talk to them, a group of local kids, who have been admiring the bicycles displayed on deck, practise cannonballs off the dock into the clear, cold water.

We explore the network of wooden steps and passages that branches off the main boardwalk and leads to the camp- ground, the dock and the hydro plant, stopping constantly to meet and talk to residents. A man leans out of a window in the band office building to tell us that ferry traffic seems to be having a generally positive effect on Klemtu, bringing in a little extra revenue and providing villagers with a welcome diversion every eight days. Another fellow explains the meaning of the artwork that decorates a dugout canoe mounted at the entrance to the dock.

Finally, it's time to return to the *Queen of Chilliwack* and settle in for the next leg of the journey, to the abandoned mill town of Ocean Falls. Dozens of villagers, who have taken advan- tage of the ferry's four-hour stopover to eat in its excellent restaurant (halibut and chips was the meal of choice) and visit its gift shop, troop off the ship. Their children reluctantly forsake the video-game machines. Peace descends upon the vessel. Before we know it, we have slipped out of Klemtu Passage and back into the main shipping channel, and returned the tiny village to its normal realm of otherworldly detachment.

Flora and Fauna

THE ANIMAL AND PLANT kingdoms of the British Columbia coast have a rich complexity that feels almost profligate. There are so many stories waiting to be told that to choose just half a dozen is to forsake entire domains. All coastal land mammals, for instance—Kermode bears and opposums and mink—will have to wait until volume two, as will insects, ferns, mosses, sea otters, western red-backed salamanders and many other deserving lifeforms.

Instead, we delve into the histories of several sentinel species: two birds, the ancient murrelet and great blue heron; one tree, the arbutus; the coastal lilies that bloom each spring; the Pacific white-sided dolphin, which has arrived in B.C. waters out of the blue; and the many races of Pacific salmon, some of which are on the verge of making a permanent exit. All are barometers, in one way or another, of how the natural world is changing.

Our dense, luxuriant rainforest, where plant grows on plant and every square centimetre of available real estate is crawling with life, appears to go on forever. The crowded subterranean gardens of the sea likewise seem abundant beyond belief. These stories, while they celebrate the vitality of our coastal ecosystems, have a cautionary element, too. B.C.'s flora and fauna are at least as fragile and as vulnerable to change as our own lives and communities are.

THE ARBUTUS

IF YOU SEARCH for the word "arbutus" in the Vancouver Public Library's computer system, the screen brings up, not a single horticultural title or nature guide, but several slim volumes of poetry. "God, when He made thee, beauteous tree, exhausted Nature's alchemy," chortled John Hosie in his 1929 chapbook *The Arbutus Tree.* Even Bret Harte, noted U.S. author of "The Outcasts of Poker Flat," "The Luck of Roaring Camp" and other short story classics, succumbed to poetic rapture when faced with the arbutus. "Never tree like thee arrayed," he wrote, "O thou gallant of the glade!"

Canada's only native broadleaf evergreen tree (known as madroña or madrone in the U.S.) seems to exert some strange power over the creative mind. I was leafing through a recent Heffel Gallery catalogue when a 1947 W.P. Weston oil, *Arbutus Shedding Bark,* caught my eye. Today, large canvases by this accomplished Vancouver artist, who died in 1967, can sell for up to $40 000. Weston loved to portray robust, solitary trees set against backdrops of muscular mountain-side. The outstretched branches of the arbutus, flesh-coloured and almost human, appear in a number of his paintings.

Those sinuous, peeling limbs, I suspect, are the tree's main attraction for most people. In early morning or evening

These Sunshine Coast arbutus trees are well established on their sunny slope. (ANDREW SCOTT)

sunlight, arbutus trunks glow with primordial energy. Their colours are surreal: the young bark chartreuse, the old bark russet, the bare wood tanned and smooth as a youthful sunbather. John Hosie saw "polished pillars... of bronze o'er-laid with cinnabar."

Father Juan Crespi, chronicler of a Spanish expedition to Monterey Bay in California, named this species "madroño" in 1769, after its resemblance to the Mediterranean madroño or strawberry tree. Archibald Menzies, naturalist on Captain Vancouver's 1792 voyage to the Pacific Northwest, made the first botanical description. In his honour, the tree was given the scientific name *Arbutus menziesii*.

There is no finer camping spot than a level arbutus grove. Auburn boughs reach toward the dappled light that filters through the tight canopy of thick, leathery foliage.

Yellowing leaves and papery tendrils of bark crackle and snap underfoot. In late spring, tiny, creamy, urn-shaped blossoms, scented like buckwheat honey, litter the forest floor. In summer, new leaves form and old ones fall to the ground. In fall, robins and varied thrushes crash through the branches to feed on bright red and orange berries, a mealy fruit also loved by mice and deer. Often perched on rocky, inhospitable bluffs, rarely found more than a few kilometres from the sea, the arbutus is to B.C.'s south coast what the sugar maple is to Quebec: an icon, a local lifeform that expresses perfectly the spirit of the land.

Related to rhododendrons, blueberries, heather and salal, arbutus is the largest member of the heath family (Ericaceae). How large? If height is the crucial criterion, then a 31.7-metre monster on Thetis Island appears to hold the current title. (A Seattle arbutus 40 metres tall, now gone, has been recorded.) Thetis can be reached by ferry from Chemainus on Vancouver Island, so off I went to see the Big Tree. Islanders directed me to a curve on Foster Point Road where the behemoth stood alone, its mossy base festooned with fresh young fronds of sword fern and loops of honeysuckle.

It was a shock to me to see an arbutus with a trunk 5 metres in circumference—as thick as an old-growth fir or cedar. However, if a stalwart stem is what defines bigness, then a Humbolt County, California, giant with a circumference of 10.36 metres has more than twice the girth of the Thetis tree. Even a 5.03-metre ancient on Savary Island outcompasses the Foster Point specimen by several centimetres. An arbutus on Esquimalt Lagoon, meanwhile, appears to have no rivals with its 23.8-metre crown spread.

But electing one specific arbutus as B.C. champion can be controversial. There are many contenders, even on Thetis Island. My Clam Bay Bed & Breakfast hostess,

Donna Kaiser, thought her neighbour's tree might be a candidate. She also sent me across the island to historic Overbury Farm, now a resort, where owner Norm Kasting kindly showed me his huge arbutus. And he knew of an even bigger one, he claimed, on the nearby property of a friend of his. To me, none seemed to match the monster I'd inspected earlier.

Everyone I talked to agreed on one thing: their trees were declining in health. "Five different stem, leaf and twig pathogens are attacking the arbutus," says Victoria arborist Don Bottrell, "as well as two species-specific insects. It's a very serious problem." Recent unusually wet winters have encouraged the growth of an insidious root rot. Many trees were also stressed during the cold, dry winter of 1989-90, leaving them susceptible to infection by fungi. The fungi spread by means of airborne spores and raise large cankers on stems and branches, which then die back, turning a burnt-looking black before finally fading to grey. Pruning and fungicides can reduce the area of infection but, often, the tree is killed.

Over the long term, arbutus could disappear from the northernmost parts of its range, where environmental pressures are greatest. Seattle's arbutus, for instance, have been seriously affected, and a grassroots replanting project is trying to help them get re-established. Arbutus are delicate and difficult to transplant, however. "They require fast-draining mineral soil," explains Harry Hill of the Native Plant Society of B.C. "They don't like soil that's too rich or moist. We've had success planting them just in sand." Their root systems are especially fragile, says Hill; if disturbed, rot quickly sets in.

The tree is also fighting a losing battle with human agencies over available coastal habitat. In the heavily populated regions surrounding Vancouver and Seattle, especially, its

numbers are in decline. Many of the locales in which it traditionally grew have now been built on or disturbed or
taken over by introduced plant species.

Arbutus is very particular about where it calls home. In
B.C., its range is mostly restricted to the shorelines of Juan
de Fuca and Georgia straits as far north as Quadra Island
and Discovery Passage. (A few isolated pockets thrive on
the west coast of Vancouver Island, at the heads of Nootka
and Barkley sounds.) The arbutus is found south as far as
California's San Diego County. A few pioneers may have
even made it across the border into Mexico. It has—for now,
anyway—one of the longest north-south ranges of any
North American tree: over 2000 kilometres.

In Oregon and California, where the species seems fairly
pathogen-resistant, arbutus is sometimes harvested for commercial purposes. The wood itself—fine-textured, dense,
with a straight or slightly wavy grain—makes beautiful floor-
ing, panelling and furniture. Young wood, which smells like
watermelon when freshly split, is light pink; with age it
darkens to dusty rose and, finally, to a rich cherry colour.
Sculptors and model builders use arbutus on occasion and
describe it as strong and brittle, tough on tools because of its
hardness but able to take a smooth, polished finish. It reacts
to changes in humidity and must be dried with care in order
to avoid cracking and warping. Arbutus also burns hot and
slow and makes excellent firewood, though putting this
noble species to such mundane use seems criminal.

First Nations people revere arbutus. In their fine guide,
Plants of Coastal British Columbia, Jim Pojar and Andy
MacKinnon tell us the Saanich tribe used its bark and leaves
as cold and stomach remedies, in a tuberculosis medicine and
for contraception. The bark was also used to colour food.
According to a Straits Salish legend, the survivors of a great

flood tied their canoe to an arbutus atop Mount Newton near Sidney on Vancouver Island. To this day, as a mark of gratitude, the Saanich do not use arbutus as firewood. Victoria poet Richard Olafson's *In Arbutus Light* refers to another Native legend, where the tree's "webbed roots hold the splintered earth together." If the arbutus should disappear, the myth warns—whether from fungal infection, habitat loss or some other cause—the planet would fly apart and be utterly destroyed.

ANCIENT MURRELETS

IN THE GATHERING DARKNESS, Jo Smith leads her little group of would-be researchers along the trail that crosses East Limestone Island. We have come ashore by Zodiac from our vessel, a handsome ketch named the *Island Roamer*, which is cruising us round the southern Queen Charlotte Islands, also known as Haida Gwaii. Smith, articulate and outgoing, is originally from Nova Scotia. She is an insect specialist, or entomologist, who has temporarily changed direction to assist Dr. Tony Gaston, a Quebec-based research scientist with the Canadian Wildlife Service, in his avian studies. Tonight, she and her colleagues will help us learn more about one of British Columbia's strangest birds: the ancient murrelet.

As we walk along, I recall my first encounter with murrelets, on Lucy Island west of Prince Rupert, out in the middle of Chatham Sound. I'd kayaked there with a friend, arriving at dusk, and was peacefully reading by flashlight when something unseen but very scary smashed against the side of the tent. I turned off the light and listened, shaking with fear, as large-sounding objects continued to thwack into the surrounding bushes. Finally, I summoned enough nerve to leave my hideout. A flashlight revealed a scene from a westcoast version of

Alice in Wonderland: legions of small birds vanishing into holes in the ground. My terror evaporated.

At the lonely outpost on East Limestone, 760 kilometres northwest of Victoria, Smith, camp supervisor Colin French and an ever changing chorus of volunteers are involved in a series of research projects. They set up camp each spring, sleep in tents, and eat and work in a tiny cedar-shingled cabin, complete with solar-powered computer and ocean view. Summers are spent on surveys of songbirds, raptors, marine mammals and the intertidal zone. Their most important study, however, focuses on *Synthliboramphus antiquus*, the ancient murrelet. Started by Dr. Gaston sixteen years ago on neighbouring Reef Island and continuing now on both islands, the program these days is organized by the Laskeek Bay Conservation Society, a local group dedicated to protecting Haida Gwaii's threatened native wildlife species. Gaston, the project's chief scientific advisor, visits occasionally from his home in Hull.

Murrelets are quail-sized, black-and-white diving birds that belong to the Alcidae family, as do auklets, murres, guillemots and puffins. Alcids, also known as auks, spend virtually their whole lives far out at sea, foraging for small fish and crustaceans. The ancient murrelet got its name because of a stripe of white feathers on the head and neck that supposedly resembles the hair of an elderly person. The species is "blue-listed," or regarded as vulnerable, by B.C.'s Ministry of Environment, Lands and Parks. The entire Canadian population—about 500 000 birds, approximately half the global total—breeds on Haida Gwaii.

(A near relative of the ancient murrelet, the marbled murrelet, became famous as a mascot and rallying cry for opponents of old-growth logging, particularly in Clayoquot Sound on Vancouver Island. This species is "red-listed," or considered imperilled, in B.C. Scientists had long suspected that the marbled murrelet only laid eggs and reared its young high up in the moss-covered branches of giant coastal evergreens, but the bird is so secretive its reproductive behaviour couldn't be confirmed conclusively until 1993, when an active nest with a chick was first discovered.)

Ancient murrelets come inland a few hundred metres to lay and incubate eggs in subterranean hollows hidden among the mossy litter of roots and fallen logs that carpets the forest floor. Like most seabirds, they are very vulnerable to predation at this time, and prefer to nest on islands, which offer the best protection against four-footed omnivores. When raccoons and rats, especially, manage to reach offshore bird nurseries, they can do incredible damage, wiping out entire colonies in short order. Forty-eight-hectare East Limestone Island is an important seabird breeding site and presently rat and raccoon free, but only because of the research team's constant vigilance.

Raccoons and rats are not native to the Queen Charlottes. Nor are squirrels, beaver, muskrats or deer, for that matter. Since their introduction to the islands by humans, all these creatures have expanded their range. Over the same period of time, native populations have declined. One endemic species, the Dawson caribou, is now extinct. Several colonies of ancient murrelets have disappeared or been drastically reduced in size. To truly appreciate the threat that introduced animals pose, it's worth making a brief digression into natural history.

The Queen Charlottes are a biological oddity. Separated from the rest of North America by the protective, eighty-kilometre-wide moat of Hecate Strait, they evolved in isolation. Many species that frequent the mainland, such as the grizzly, fisher, chipmunk and mink, did not reach the archipelago. Parts of Haida Gwaii probably escaped the relentless glacial destruction of the last ice age, providing areas of refuge for some creatures. Through adaptation over many millenia to an island environment, a number of new species and subspecies emerged: mosses and lichens, insects, plants, sticklebacks, mice and shrews. Larger, more complex life-forms—the Steller's jay, saw-whet owl, hairy woodpecker, ermine, marten, caribou and black bear—also altered ancient bloodlines and diverged to form varieties found nowhere else on the planet.

Competition from introduced species now threatens these and other native animals and plants in the Queen Charlottes. This pattern is the bane of island ecosystems everywhere. Non-native predators wiped out thirteen kinds of the ostrich-like moa in New Zealand, the dodo on Mauritius, Madagascar's elephant bird... you get the idea. The list of casualties is lengthy. Of 176 bird species known to have become extinct over the last 400 years, 93 percent were native to islands. Rats, dogs and human beings, all recent arrivals to the islands in question, were heavily implicated in the birds' demise.

Predators are not the only problem facing insular ecosystems. Sheep and goats, often deposited by sailors as future sources of food, have caused untold damage to countless islands. Non-native herbivores destroy habitat needed by native species and compete with them for food. As we cross East Limestone Island, we pause to marvel at the trunks of Sitka spruce rising around us like giant spears in the dim light. Jo Smith points out how little undergrowth there is. It's the black-tailed deer, she explains, which were introduced to Haida Gwaii over eighty-five years ago and have since multiplied like rabbits. They nibble everything right down to the ground; the young spruce are cropped back so regularly they look dwarfed, like stunted bonsai trees. Researchers on Limestone and elsewhere in the Charlottes are looking at methods of deer control and comparing vegetation recovery rates in deer-infested areas with rates in areas where deer have been excluded.

As we resume our tour, Smith shows us several ancient murrelet burrows her team is monitoring. Inconspicuous heat sensors, which register a higher burrow temperature when the parent birds are present, have been carefully inserted next to selected nests. The female murrelet lays one enormous egg, says Smith, then leaves it for eight to ten days before returning to the burrow to lay a second one. Together, the two eggs equal almost half her body weight. The parents take turns incubating these whoppers for a month or so, and then the young birds, which both hatch at about the same time, slowly peck their way out of their shells. This can take four days or more.

The plentiful supply of nutrients stored in the giant eggs enables murrelet chicks to come into the world almost fully developed, covered with thick down and cute as can be. This precocial condition of birth is a rare phenomenon, and as Tony Gaston points out in his detailed book, *The Ancient Murrelet: A Natural History in the Queen Charlotte Islands*, it offers scientists a paradox. Why has such a survival strategy been overlooked by other types of birds, which usually spend weeks rearing their helpless offspring? What makes this alternative evolutionary pathway feasible for ancient murrelets?

A day or two after the chicks have hatched, the adult birds leave the nests at night, assemble offshore and call to them. The tennis ball-sized hatchlings scamper out of the burrows, stumble and clamber their way over logs and rocks and down slopes to the water, where they swim out to miraculous reunions with the appropriate moms and pops. Then they are led well away from land to enjoy, at last, their first meal.

Scamper time usually happens in May, which is why we're here. A long sheet of plastic has been ingeniously placed where it will funnel the chicks so we can gently collect and help weigh, measure and band them. With lots of chicks banded—and with additional data gathered by re-examining the adult birds at nesting time—a detailed profile of the species is being built up. A great deal has already been learned about murrelet reproduction and mortality rates, age distribution and population size. But their strange lifestyle still leaves much to be revealed. Where do the birds spend the winter, for instance? What are their migration patterns? How are murrelets and other pelagic birds affected by ocean disturbances such as the last El Niño?

Dr. Gaston believes that the species' unusual reproductive strategy, with the precocial chicks and the rapid departure to the ocean, evolved in response to its high mortality rate on land, where the clumsy birds are easy prey. Only 75 percent of breeding adults survive from year to year, the lowest figure recorded for any pelagic bird. Ancient murrelets, however, also have the highest recorded birth rate, about 1.5 chicks per breeding pair. (Most seabirds lay a single egg; carrying food back and forth takes up so much energy that one chick is all they can manage to raise.) Even so, such fecundity can only be maintained if the chicks are taken to the food rather than vice versa, a practice that also reduces the risk of predation.

While waiting to meet the amazing murrelet chicks face to face, we chat with Colin French, a Haida Gwaii veteran, who tells us how he helped exterminate rats on Langara, the most northerly Queen Charlotte island. This project, one of the largest of its type ever undertaken, has largely succeeded in reclaiming Langara for its original seabird inhabitants, which had been driven away by the proliferating rodents. Limestone's current volunteers—Charlie, a youthful banding specialist all the way from England; Ken, a university student from Calgary; Beth, who is pursuing hummingbirds for a graduate degree; and Christy, an itinerant veterinarian—wander by and join in the conversation. Despite the discomforts of the bush and the fact that much of their work is done at night, everyone seems to be having a grand time.

The researcher's life, however, is fraught with uncertainty as well as inconvenience. It turns out that we're too early. The chicks won't be leaving their burrows tonight, after all. Maybe tomorrow night. But by then we'll be far away, marvelling over a pod of grey whales as they repeatedly dive for food on the ocean floor.

But that's another story.

PACIFIC WHITE-SIDED DOLPHINS

MY GOD! SOMEONE YELLS, pointing to a commotion on the ocean surface half a kilometre away. Within seconds the splashes resolve into a dozen sleek, curved shapes that streak directly towards our vessel with disconcerting speed. But the streamlined torpedoes about to intercept us are not armed. They are Pacific white-sided dolphins. With child-like glee they leap beside the boat, seemingly thrilled to encounter a group of middle-aged ecotourists.

We're thrilled, too, and surprised. I'd had no idea dolphins could even be found in Pacific Northwest coastal waters. Over the decades, I'd glimpsed a few killer whales, one false killer whale, three harbour porpoises and two schools of cheerful black-and-white Dall's porpoises, another boat-loving species that roostertails through the ocean like a shark in a low-budget movie. But dolphins? Not a single one.

For the next thirty minutes the white-sides play around us. They are small by dolphin standards, about the length and weight of football players. Their grey backs glisten as they surf our nine-knot bow wave and gambol in the wake. As we lean over the gunwales to watch their acrobatic forms zigzag back and forth beneath the hull, we can almost reach out and touch them. They jump up to two metres out

Pacific white-sided dolphins are amazing oceanic gymnasts. (ALEXANDRA MORTON)

of the water, regarding us with bemused expressions as they hang in the sunshine. They seem to be smiling.

Everyone aboard is smiling back. We enter a trance, absorbed by this joyous intelligence erupting from the dark waters. Day-to-day preoccupations disappear. We are being visited, it seems—contacted, even—by another sentient creature. Eventually the dolphins tire of our presence and disappear, leaving us almost exhausted.

There is something unforgettable about spotting dolphins in the wild; the memory lingers on a deep level of the psyche. Dolphins have a potent effect on the human imagination. We see them as symbols of freedom, joy and spontaneity. Their story, for once, is not about impending extinction. On the contrary, dolphins seem to be returning to the Pacific Northwest coast. I've encountered them several times since

1996: in Johnstone Strait and Burke Channel, and in south-east Alaska's Behm Canal. Why are they here?

The person to talk to if you want to learn more about Pacific white-sided dolphins is Kathy Heise, a forty-year-old post-graduate researcher in the zoology department at the University of British Columbia. Heise had been working as a lighthouse keeper on B.C.'s central coast for five years when, in 1986, she saw several hundred of the animals passing through Johnstone Strait. Intrigued to spot a species that supposedly inhabits only offshore waters, she began to search for more information and found very little. This deficiency led her to UBC and a 1996 master's thesis on the "life history parameters" of that ocean charmer, *Lagenorhynchus obliquidens*.

For her thesis, Heise observed the behaviour of white-sided dolphins on ninety-two occasions. She measured dive times and made hydrophone recordings. She videotaped her subjects, hoping to identify individuals by their markings, as has been done with B.C.'s killer whales. With a long-handled net, she painstakingly retrieved fragments left over from feeding sessions to see what was on the dolphin menu (herring and salmon mostly).

Heise knew from reading and from interviews that dolphins had been encountered on and off in coastal waters over the years. Archaeological evidence, gleaned from thousand-year-old middens or refuse heaps of First Nations people, indicates that dolphins and other marine mammals were important food sources at times, though never as vital as salmon.

She distributed a questionnaire to 500 mariners. When and where had they first seen dolphins? she asked. How many had they seen? Did they think that populations were increasing or declining? Her survey suggested that the animals had rarely been noted inshore before 1984. In the

1980s, they were observed more frequently in central and northern coastal waters. In the 1990s, they have been spied in the Strait of Georgia as close to Vancouver as Horseshoe Bay. In fact, Pacific white-sided dolphins may now be more abundant in B.C. than any other cetacean.

Heise proves difficult to interview because she's often away, bobbing around various mid-coast sounds on a small boat borrowed from the Vancouver Aquarium. While waiting for her to surface, I look into the literature on dolphins. My curiosity is nothing new. Over the centuries, our interest in these creatures has bordered on obsession. We have stitched them into our myths and folk tales, invested them with supernatural powers. To the early cultures of the Mediterranean, dolphins were auspicious animals, released when caught in fishermen's nets. Their images appear on coins, ceramics and 3600-year-old Minoan frescoes.

Humankind has made the dolphin its aquatic alter ego. Dolphins are mammals, after all, warm-blooded and air-breathing. They are roughly the same size as us. They mate as we do. They suckle their young. Both species are social, curious, playful, communicative. Both are aggressive towards their own kind as well as other animals. A dolphin has almost as much brain matter per kilogram as a human.

Dolphins appear to search us out, chasing after our boats. According to Greek legend, in their former lives they had *been* human. The gods changed them into marine mammals for their evil deeds and they made amends, supposedly, by leading vessels to safety and rescuing lost swimmers.

These animals are symbols of rebirth and also of sexuality. "Venus among the fishes skips and is a she-dolphin," wrote D.H. Lawrence. Chilean writer Isabel Allende tells the story of a female friend who signed up to swim with a dolphin. The creature ripped her bathing suit to shreds with his male organ, then made two circuits of the pool "balancing on his tail," while she, naked, "was fished out kicking and churning in a net before the astonished eyes of the other participants."

Much of what we know about dolphins comes courtesy of the bottlenose, a large, acrobatic species that can be bred and trained in captivity. Most aquarium dolphins are bottlenoses, as was Flipper (played by several bottlenoses, in fact). There are more than thirty types of dolphins in all, including a number of Asian and South American river dwellers. They vary in size and hue from the tiny 1.2-metre vaquita, found only in Mexico's Gulf of California, to the 4-metre grampus, or Risso's dolphin, with its scarred body and bulging forehead, which roams all of the world's temperate and tropical oceans.

People believe amazing things about dolphins: they are here to help the human race evolve; they are telepathic; they come from a water planet near Sirius. Certainly the "intelligence" of dolphins—their quickness to learn, skill as mimics and wide vocal range—has attracted much attention. The U.S. Navy considered them as potential aquatic saboteurs. Some who have swum with dolphins credit them with healing powers of compassion.

Scientists try not to identify emotionally with the creatures they are observing. But even they can succumb, says Kathy Heise, when I catch up to her, to the allure of dolphins. Hale complexion, dark hair tied back, Heise has the air of someone who's spent many twenty-hour days out on the water. "I'm never grumpy when I watch dolphins," she admits, "so I guess that's emotional. I'm very intrigued by them. But in order to be most open to what I can learn, I've had to cut back on the anthropomorphizing."

Heise has spent years pondering the appearance of dolphins in B.C. waters. "The most logical explanation," she says, "is population growth." Estimates of their numbers vary wildly, from tens of thousands to four million or more. If the species were experiencing population growth, it would be forced to expand its range. But by analyzing birth rates and ages, calving intervals, and fertility and gestation periods, Heise concluded that the population was stationary or, at best, growing very slowly.

The next theory she examined held that the animals had been driven out of the open ocean by the calamitous driftnet fishery. Fifty to ninety thousand white-sided dolphins are known to have been killed in the North Pacific between 1978 and 1990 by the multi-kilometre-long nets towed by Asian fishing boats ostensibly searching for squid. The problem with this explanation is that driftnets were outlawed in 1992, and B.C.'s dolphins have remained inshore.

The most likely explanation involves "regime shifts": large, poorly understood oceanographic and climate changes that affect water temperatures and the distribution of fish. Scientists believe they have identified at least four climate regimes that affect the North Pacific: a short two- or three-year cycle; the famous El Niño/La Niña event, or southern oscillation, which lasts three to seven years; the Pacific decadal oscillation, or PDO, with a period of twenty to thirty years; and a very low frequency rotation of fifty to seventy-five years. Certainly, a major shift from cooler to warmer conditions began off the B.C. coast in 1976, reversing a warm-to-cool trend that had started almost thirty years earlier.

Dolphins, being opportunistic feeders, go where they can. Sockeye and pink salmon in B.C. have actually multiplied in recent years, even as coho and chinook stocks have shrunk. Pilchards, or Pacific sardines—which formed an important provincial fishery from the 1920s to 1940s, then disappeared—have returned to our waters. Mackerel, rarely seen fifteen years ago, now appear plentiful. Populations of major prey species such as mackerel, hake, pilchard and capelin are believed to fluctuate in ocean regime-related cycles. "Maybe the dolphins moved inshore," speculates Heise, "found that food was readily available and decided to stay." B.C. waters, however, are due for a long-term cooling oscillation. Heise's thesis suggests that Pacific white-sided dolphins primarily like warm waters. So they may not stick around. No one really knows.

That's the word from the science desk: very strange things are going on out in the ocean. Talking to Heise reminds me that while our actions and beliefs have huge impacts on the natural world, we know little about that world's deeper rhythms. For those of us who have grown up in cities, where every surface has been refashioned and most natural cycles tamed, it's all too easy to ignore the greater life that surges around us. We even forget we are part of a larger system.

Strangely, I haven't seen a single wild dolphin since first meeting Heise in 1998. I hear about their exploits, though, their amazing speed, their breathtaking aerial displays. Fastest and most active of the dolphins, Pacific white-sides are able to reach speeds of twenty-five knots—about forty-five kilometres per hour. They somersault end over end. They flip like gymnasts. Schools of a thousand animals have been spotted repeatedly leaping and falling back onto the surface with coordinated splashes. Larger schools—more than 5000 strong—form solid kilometre-wide walls and have been mistaken by observers for oncoming storms. Like other dolphins, white-sides feed cooperatively. They use their astonishing echolocation skills (a blindfolded animal can locate a golf ball a hundred metres away) to herd or circle fish so they can be caught more easily. Their only predators in B.C. are "transient," marine mammal-eating killer whales. They live into their forties.

To stave off dolphin withdrawal pangs, I go down to the Vancouver Aquarium Marine Science Centre in Stanley Park and watch Whitewings, a Pacific white-sided specimen who has been an ambassador for her species for over twenty-five years. I admire her black beak and distinct white chin, the dark line where the subtle greys of her back meet the gleaming white flanks. She has fearlessly shared quarters with a series of giant killer-whale cousins. Now she and Bjossa, her sole surviving poolmate, play together, chasing each other about and swimming side by side.

By all accounts congenial, Whitewings can hardly be expected to symbolize joyous spontaneity, as wild dolphins do. Despite the frisky jumps and tricks for fish rewards, her dolphin smile seems worn. After a quarter-century in her concrete-and-glass bowl, I wonder if she even remembers the watery world beyond. Round and round she goes, eating the same food, every day. No choice in the matter. Like many Vancouver residents, Whitewings is trapped on an endless urban treadmill.

In the 1960s, neurologist John Lilly suggested that dolphins used language and that we could communicate with them. But we're not communicating with them. In the 1970s, Jacques Cousteau believed that dolphins could be domesticated to "become our great helpmate in the sea, the equivalent of the horse on land." His idea would be scorned today.

Yet dolphins may still be able to help us. They can remind us of how out of touch we are with nature—and how we need to reawaken our dolphin spirits. "A lot of people have a special connection with dolphins and whales," says Kathy Heise. "If it makes them more concerned about what is going on in the marine environment, I think that's great."

SPRING LILIES

ONE RITUAL OF SPRING in our household is an expedition to see wild lilies in bloom. There is something magical about these native plants, which flower so early in the season, so suddenly, and for such a brief period of time. Their exotic shapes and colours never fail to amaze me. It seems right that such delicate beauty should take a little effort to uncover. For us, a boat ride is required, to a cluster of islets off a point of land near our Sunshine Coast home. It is only there, on sunny, south-facing ledges, that the lilies seem to flourish. We usually kayak over. Often, it's the first paddle of the year.

While many members of the lily family grow in B.C., we see only three species on our offshore pilgrimage. The first is the chocolate lily, a fritillary, whose unusual floral bells are dark purple, mottled with chequered patterns of yellow, green and brown. Then there's the common camas, with its brilliant blue, star-shaped petals. Both these plants were important food sources for First Nations people, and it seems ironic that the third lily we find here, growing right next to the others, is highly poisonous: meadow death-camas, its creamy-white blooms clustered at the top of a tall stem.

At one time, lilies were far more abundant in the region than they are today. Meriwether Lewis, who with his partner, William Clark, made one of the earliest explorations of western North America, had the good fortune to see camas meadows before the advent of agriculture and suburbs. A June 12, 1806, entry in his journal reads: "The quawmash is now in blume and... at a short distance it resembles lakes of fine clear water, so complete in this deseption that on first sight I could have sworn it was water." (The word camas has many variant spellings.)

Beauty and frequent edibility seem to be the hallmarks of the lily family, Liliaceae, which is large and international. Onions, garlic, leeks and asparagus belong to it, as do tulips, hyacinths and hostas. At least thirty family members are native to the B.C. coast, including trillium, brodiaea, queen's cup, Indian hellebore and several types of wild onion.

Some of the showiest species, such as the yellow glacier and white avalanche lilies, as well as the more demure alp lily, prefer higher ground, as their names suggest. That still leaves plenty of springtime spectacle for the lower altitudes. There's the tiger lily, B.C.'s only "true" lily or member of the *Lilium* genus, with its extravagant orange, purple-dotted flowers. The delicate fawn or Easter lily comes in both pink and white forms. And the black lily, or northern rice root, which grows from Washington to Alaska, has striking bronze or purple-brown blossoms.

Many lily species were gathered for food by First Nations groups, but camas bulbs, in particular, were a dietary staple for Coast Salish and other tribes, and also an important trade item. The cultivation and tending of camas meadows were as close to agriculture as west-coast Native people got. Prime camas beds were the property of certain families and passed on through inheritance. Other fields were available for public harvest. Each season, the beds were weeded and cleared of stones and death-camas plants; brush was eliminated with a controlled annual burn.

Nancy Turner, a leading ethnobotanist and professor of environmental studies at the University of Victoria, has spent years studying how camas was harvested and prepared. Women, she says, usually dug the bulbs with hard, pointed sticks of yew or ocean spray (ironwood). Entire families would participate in the harvest, which took place in early summer, just before the flowers faded, and could last for weeks. The bulbs were at their biggest then, and the common camas could easily be distinguished from death-camas. The turf was cut and lifted out, then replaced after the larger bulbs had been plucked; small ones were left for next season. Some Coast Salish groups replanted the ripe seed capsules. It wasn't unusual for a tireless family to gather as much as 200 kilograms of camas annually.

Explorer and botanist David Douglas, who travelled through the Pacific Northwest in the 1820s and '30s, described in his journal how the plant was cooked. A fire was lit in a large pit lined with flat stones. When the stones were red hot, the ashes were removed and the stones covered with leaves, moss and seaweed. Large quantities of camas, up to fifty kilograms or more, were added, then more vegetation, then a layer of earth. A hole was made with a stick and water poured in, and the bulbs were left to steam and bake for up to thirty-six hours. "When warm," Douglas reported, "they taste much like a baked pear.... Assuredly they produce flatulence: when in the Indian hut I was almost blown out by strength of wind."

Camas bulbs consist mostly of inulin, a complex form of sugar; a lengthy baking process was necessary to reduce this indigestible carbohydrate to a more palatable form—fructose.

The cooked bulbs were notably sweet. Most were con-
sumed immediately, often at a ceremonial feast. Some were
used for sweetening other foods or were pressed into bis-
cuits or loaves and sun-dried for trade or storage. Black and
chocolate lily bulbs contained a more starchy type of carbohydrate and were usually prepared by being boiled briefly in
wooden or woven containers.

John Jewitt, an English sailor held captive by the
Nuu-chah-nulth at Nootka Sound in the early 1800s, called
camas "a very fine vegetable, being sweet, mealy, and of a
most agreeable flavour." It was regarded by some groups
almost as a confection. Not everyone agreed with Jewitt,
however. An 1890 U.S. census document referred to the
"sickening" taste of camas. "It is liked by Indians," the
report went on, "and will fatten hogs, making very fine
flavored meats, but it is not palatable to a white man."
George Simpson of the Hudson's Bay Company called camas
"a poor and nauseous food."

Camas ranges from southern B.C. to California and into
eastern Washington, Oregon and Idaho. Wherever it grew,
it was esteemed by Native people, and the camas trade
extended as far as Montana, Alberta and the central B.C.
coast. In northeastern Oregon, the plant even played a role in
a bitter 1877 war between Chief Joseph of the Nez Percé and
the U.S. government. White settlers ploughed up rich camas
fields in the Wallowa Valley, and the destruction of this ancient
resource was regarded by Joseph as an act of such wanton
stupidity as to be beyond understanding or forgiveness.

By the 1930s, the Aboriginal use of lily bulbs had all but
disappeared. Various recipes for camas—mashed up in a
thick soup, dressed with eulachon grease or whale oil,
served with chunks of deer meat or salmon in a stew, boiled
down to a rich brown syrup like molasses—are preserved

in oral histories, but today, only the elderly can recall the aromatic, nutty flavour of the bulbs. "Oh, it was sweet," one Nitinaht woman told Nancy Turner in the early 1980s. "I still miss it."

The Garry oak meadows of southern Vancouver Island and the Gulf Islands are home to some incredibly productive camas grounds. In certain traditional digging areas, such as Victoria's Beacon Hill Park, the beds still contain as many as 200 plants per square metre. Researchers such as Brenda Beckwith, a doctoral student at the University of Victoria, now believe that these "meadow" landscapes are not natural at all but have resulted from centuries of cultivation and management by Native people. Historical reports compared the site of Fort Victoria to an English park, calling it "a work of art" and "a perfect Eden." Without the Coast Salish, says Beckwith, this "garden" might never have come into existence.

It would be difficult to revitalize the use of camas as a Native food. The Garry oak/camas meadows are in rapid decline today. Since the arrival of white settlers, foraging livestock have decimated many lily beds, and the open, prairie-like habitat is ideal for human developments of all types. The International Garry Oak Meadow Symposium and Community Festival, held in Victoria in May every few years, attempts to focus attention on the plight of this disappearing ecosystem, and the Garry Oak Meadows Preservation Society is trying to protect what's left of it.

These efforts are beginning to produce results: several important oak/camas habitats have been saved recently—at Maple Bay near Duncan, on South Winchelsea Island north of Nanaimo and on Russell Island south of Saltspring. At Mount Tolmie Park in Victoria, and at other sites, volunteers are working to rid lily meadows of broom, an invasive introduced shrub.

It's not surprising that a cult of dedicated fanciers and horticulturalists has grown up around lilies, including camas. Because of their scarcity, lily bulbs should never be removed from the wild (even indiscriminate tromping through the meadows can damage them). Some of the more spectacular species can be grown from seed, and many plant nurseries now carry native lilies. According to Richard Fraser, of Fraser's Thimble Farm on Saltspring Island, common camas and black and tiger lilies are the easiest to propagate. "From a commercial standpoint," says Fraser, "lilies are a very slow crop. We're looking at four to eight years before they bloom." A white variety of the blue camas is now available, as well.

B.C. lilies are popular ornamentals in Europe, courtesy of David Douglas, who introduced many species to England after his travels. Indeed, when the chefs at Vancouver Island's Sooke Harbour House got the idea of serving camas at their famed restaurant, they first had to order plants from Holland. Now they grow them in their own gardens. The bulbs are pressure-cooked and presented as a soup or a side vegetable. "People would be just as happy with mashed potatoes, believe it or not," says chef Brock Windsor. "But we make them eat the stuff and they seem to be quite pleased with it."

GREAT BLUE HERONS

BOB FORRESTER LEADS me to a trail at the north edge of Cooper's Green, a waterfront park in Halfmoon Bay on the Sunshine Coast. The light grows dim as we get deeper into the woods, and the path soon disappears, replaced by an intricate groundcover of lacy herb Robert leaves. A stream meanders through this part of the park, and a grove of mixed red alder, red cedar and bigleaf maple has sprung up to take advantage of the moisture.

"There," says Forrester, stopping and pointing up into the canopy. "There they are." Twenty metres or more above us, wedged into the crowns of a group of mature alders and almost hidden in the greenery, I can see several bristling, metre-wide bundles of twigs and branches: great blue heron nests. We count at least five of these dense brown baskets. Other, older nests have fallen to the ground beneath the trees. Even though it's the end of June, when a heron colony should be rollicking with the raucous cries of hungry chicks and the hoarse croaks of pressured, food-fetching adults, the only sound we hear, shrill and incessant, is the complaint of a bald eagle.

"Three pairs of herons came in early spring," reports Forrester, who lives next door to Cooper's Green. "They

A group of nearly fledged great blue heron chicks await their next meal in Vancouver's Pacific Spirit Park. (ROSS VENNESLAND)

looked well settled, and everything seemed to be going great." But at the end of May, after the chicks had hatched, he heard "a god awful racket" at the colony and went over to investigate. The adult herons were circling the nests, obviously distraught. Later the birds disappeared, and Forrester hasn't seen them at the nesting site since. He believes bald eagles drove off the adults and killed the chicks. We feel a mutual sense of loss as we stare up at the empty nests, for this had been the last active great blue heron colony in the area.

A few days before, I'd plunged into a stand of Douglas firs at Tuwanek on the east shore of Sechelt Inlet and found three more heron nests that had been occupied earlier in the 1999 breeding season. The forest was silent. Beneath the nests were fresh shell fragments from the herons' pale blue eggs, indicating that clutches had been laid and nestlings hatched. But this colony, like the one at Cooper's Green, was deserted.

Over the previous week, I'd checked all the known nest-ing sites around the Sunshine Coast and Powell River, assisting a Simon Fraser University graduate student, Ross Vennesland, with his research into why great blue herons abandon nesting colonies. Wherever I went, the herons were gone. By talking to people who lived close by, I found that, in most locations, the birds had been absent for sever-al years. Yet, as recently as a decade ago, this part of British Columbia was a prolific breeding ground for the species. In 1979, forty-four active heron nests were counted at Pender Harbour and another thirty-five at Sechelt. In 1990, thirty-eight occupied nests were noted at Powell River. In July 1999, the tally for the entire region was exactly zero.

The earlier data had been gathered by Robert Butler, a Canadian Wildlife Service biologist and Vennesland's thesis supervisor. Butler summarized years of painstaking research in a 1997 book, *The Great Blue Heron*, which is both a natural history and a plea for conservation. B.C.'s herons are under threat, he wrote. "Urban sprawl has con-sumed quiet woodlots where the heron nests, its eggs and tissues contain contaminants from industrial, agricultural and residential developments, and its nesting sites are increasingly disturbed by eagles and human activities." Yet great blue herons remain a familiar sight, dear to the hearts of coastal residents.

An iconic species, these birds evoke the spirit of the land as few other animals can. Who has not paused to admire the patience of a stalking heron? Here is nature's ballet: the slow-motion stretch of the leg, the silky forward glide of the neck. A heron at work is an ideal example of concentration without effort, the avian equivalent of a Tai Chi master or one of those "human sculpture" performance artists, whose movements are so smooth and imperceptible you can hardly follow them. To watch a heron hunt focuses the mind; the absorption of the bird seems transferred to the observer. Time and space dissolve. There is just the heron and its unseen prey.

Herons inspire us. As I drove around checking nest sites, I became aware that heron art is everywhere. In front of a Tuwanek guesthouse, a heron sculpture stands sentry in the garden. A fine painted image marks Sechelt's Blue Heron Inn. Embedded in the sidewalk of Powell River's main street, multicoloured strips of metal cleverly outline a heron. A flip through the phonebook reveals Blue Heron Software, Blue Heron Cabinets and a Blue Heron antique store. The bird was revered by First Nations groups, too, and depicted on masks and amulets. One of the earliest carvings found at the Marpole archaeological site on the Fraser River has a heron shape.

There are about sixty species of heron in the world. Taxonomists list four varieties, or subspecies, of the great blue heron. One inhabits the Galapagos Islands; another, pure white in colour, lives around the Gulf of Mexico; a third roams most of continental North America; the fourth, found only in the Pacific Northwest, is our own familiar bird—*Ardea herodias fannini.*

Herons may appear plentiful, probably because they prefer the mild, urbanized southwest corner of the province, as we do, and seem to tolerate our presence. But they are not. Rob Butler estimates that B.C. is home to only about 2400 nesting pairs, a number that includes the 400 pairs that forage on the Fraser River delta but nest in the huge Point Roberts colony just across the border in the U.S. The species is considered "vulnerable and at risk" by provincial authorities.

Herons feed mostly on small fish such as gunnels, sculpins and shiner perch. They also catch shrimp, crabs, frogs, shrews and voles. The eelgrass meadows on the mudflats of the Fraser estuary are especially important to them, as millions of fingerlings congregate there in spring. Herons gather at such sites in March and April to select new mates for the season. Their appearance changes at this time of year; elaborate plumes are grown on the breast, and yellow bills turn almost orange. Courting herons indulge in a variety of displays, most of which show off their new finery.

Mated birds raise chicks in treetop colonies that range in size from a handful of nests to several hundred. Some herons refurbish old nests; others build new ones. Three to five eggs, slightly larger than those of a chicken, are laid, and both parents share incubation duties, which take about twenty-eight days. With stout beaks and bushy, grey top-knots, young chicks appear rather comical (although their parents might disagree). They grow fast. In two weeks they can stand. After four, they are hopping about on nearby branches and flapping their wings. Young herons are almost fully grown by week six and leave the nest after two months—often in mid-July. In two years they will be ready to breed. Adults can live to be twenty-three.

It's early July by the time I finally get to see a live colony. Ross Vennesland kindly lets me tag along when he visits the one hidden in Vancouver's Pacific Spirit Park near the University of British Columbia. We hear the herons long before we see them. The constant *guk-guk-guk* sound of the chicks rises to a frantic crescendo whenever an adult arrives with food. My guide ascribes one ear-splitting, colony-wide eruption to an eagle's approach, though I see nothing.

Vennesland's work this morning involves counting chicks with a spotting scope and setting up an infrared "trip wire" in order to track human and animal intruders. While he labours, I wander into the thicket of alders where the colony is located. The smell is astonishing: an ammonia-and-dead-fish odour that lingers in the memory and the clothing. The giant prehistoric silhouettes of adult birds float overhead every few minutes, circling, landing and then leaving again.

The chicks are the same size as their parents: over two kilograms in weight, with a wingspan of two metres. I can see them clearly in the canopy, high above. Walking on the soggy ground beneath the nests is hazardous. White liquid excrement rains down, and the carcasses of dead chicks—feathers, legs, bones; some recent, some decayed—lie strewn on the dying vegetation. A garnish of rotting fish provides the finishing touch to this macabre charnel house. For young herons, survival is a long shot: many fall from their nests; others are pushed off or outmanoeuvred for food by older siblings. And there is the constant danger of predators.

The UBC colony, Vennesland explains, is one of the largest in B.C., having grown over the past few years to 190 active nests. But only 60 of them, he believes, will actually fledge chicks this year. The colony's productivity is low: half a chick per nest on average, compared to two or two and a half per nest in more stable colonies. "Bald eagles are the reason for all that," he says. "The big questions are: why are eagle attacks increasing, and why are they only attacking certain colonies?"

It is the coastal colonies that are bearing the brunt of eagle predation, according to Vennesland's research. The Sunshine Coast is a heron wasteland. Vancouver Island and environs are down from fifteen colonies to four, with only two—at Duncan and on Saltspring Island—expected to have high reproductive success. The UBC colony is hurting. The colony at Sidney Island in the Strait of Georgia, where Rob Butler gathered much of the data for his book, was deserted in 1990 after numerous eagle strikes. And a huge, 400-nest colony at Birch Bay in Washington state was abandoned in 1999 for the same reason, leaving one lonely pair of adults trying to raise their beleaguered offspring. Heron colonies further inland, however, such as a large one on the Canadian Forces Base at Chilliwack, are doing fine.

In *The Great Blue Heron,* Butler notes that bald eagle numbers have climbed 30 percent over the last decade. They continue to grow. Bald eagles prefer to feed on fish, but fish populations are in decline everywhere on the Pacific coast. Vennesland speculates that eagles may be turning to other food sources, such as heron chicks. (Attacks are also up on seabirds.) Another theory suggests that eagle numbers were unnaturally low in recent years, and are now recovering. During this period, herons expanded their range; now they are paying the price. Vennesland's studies focus on colony size; while there is safety in numbers, he finds, immense colonies also attract large numbers of predators. Both Butler and Vennesland theorize that herons will form smaller colonies in the future, in hopes of minimizing attacks.

Herons and eagles may have been struggling over territory for millenia, like characters in some great epic. Large-scale human disturbance, however, is a more recent phenomenon. Individual birds, or groups of birds, often adapt well to our presence—a colony flourished for years in a well-patronized part of Stanley Park, for instance—but nesting habitat is being lost rapidly in southwestern B.C. A 1990 Canadian Wildlife Service report found that for every thousand new human arrivals to the lower Fraser Valley, twenty-eight hectares of rural land are converted to urban use.

In 1997, Butler helped launch the Heron Stewardship Program, which encourages private and public landowners to protect habitat used by the birds. "It's doing well," he explains two years later. "All the big colonies have some kind of protected status." The land that the Saltspring Island and Point Roberts colonies nest on has actually been bought by helpful organizations. In 1999, the Chilliwack colony became part of a district nature sanctuary.

For Rob Butler, the great blue heron is a bellwether species for conservation efforts in the Strait of Georgia region. Because it is found throughout this rapidly changing landscape, the heron can be viewed as a symbol for the health of the entire ecosystem. It forages in the streams and on the marshes, mudflats and grasslands; it nests in the mature forests. If the heron thrives, so might we. But if it dies out, we will surely also be in trouble.

SALMON STRAINS

AT A REFRIGERATED bull-semen depository in Langley, fisheries biologist Dr. Brian Harvey is creating an insurance policy for British Columbia's wild salmon. Since 1993, First Nations groups working with Harvey's World Fisheries Trust have been gathering sperm samples from endangered salmon stocks and saving them in the cold-storage facility. They are doing this so it might be possible to rebuild dying runs of fish in the future if conditions for their survival happen to improve. The process is a slow one. Only a few dozen of the thousands of genetically distinct varieties of salmon that exist on Canada's West Coast are represented in the International Fisheries Gene Bank, as the modest collection is boldly named.

The bank is one of many initiatives undertaken by the Victoria-based Trust on behalf of B.C.'s beleaguered salmon and in the name of sustainable fisheries everywhere. As its name implies, the nonprofit organization has a global outlook. The Trust hosted a 1998 international conference on aquatic biodiversity and is assisting the United Nations' Food and Agriculture Organization to develop sustainable fisheries policies. Brian Harvey, an intense, energetic fifty-one-year-old, is often on the road. In fact, he writes a

Biologist Brian Harvey directs the worldwide conservation efforts of Victoria's World Fisheries Trust. (Courtesy World Fisheries Trust)

column for the *Victoria Times Colonist* on the humorous travails of a travelling scientist. I track him down at World Fisheries Trust headquarters, a small suite in a refurbished brick office building on Fisgard Street in Chinatown.

He deftly describes for me how gene banking works. From every stock selected for the program, fifty male salmon are briefly detained at spawning time. Fieldworkers gently squeeze a spoonful of creamy liquid milt from each fish, which is then released unharmed. A pinch of cryoprotectant is added to the semen, and it's then poured into plastic straws and placed in a large insulated container, where liquid nitrogen will gradually cool the sperm cells to almost -200° Celsius.

Back in Langley, the straws are transferred to permanent storage, where they may remain for decades. Harvey would prefer they never be thawed out, for each withdrawal would be a desperate gesture—an indication that a race of salmon was in serious trouble. Unfortunately, hundreds of stocks are already extinct in B.C. and hundreds more are headed towards extinction. "If we keep marching along this road," says the Chicago-born biologist, who earned his doctorate and worked for a number of years at the University of Victoria, "the species may ultimately not be able to adapt to such threats as climate change and habitat destruction because adaptability is edited out every time a stock is lost." His gene bank, therefore, is a last resort.

The World Fisheries Trust has also been active in South America in recent years. In Brazil, where migratory fish—including some unusual giant catfish and other important food species—are threatened by dam-building, Harvey has been working with local scientists, helping them assess the dangers inherent in hydroelectric development and teaching them gene-banking techniques and fish-ladder design. Closer to home, the trust is involved in several Canadian projects. Harvey shows me slides of a watershed restoration underway at Tseycum Creek in the Kootenays and a salmon enumeration fence being constructed at Kirby Creek in Sooke on Vancouver Island. He talks mostly, however, about the main focus of his organization, which has always been the preservation of Pacific salmon stocks.

Over the centuries, he explains, each stock—and by a stock, biologists mean a race or subgroup of a species associated with one particular river—develops its own genetic "fingerprint." Because salmon use their remarkable homing instincts to return to specific spawning grounds, and rarely interbreed with other stocks, the separation between races eventually becomes fairly extreme—more pronounced, in fact, than with any other species of fish. Chinook stocks from two adjacent streams can differ radically in size, shape, colour and temperament. The West Coast of North

America is home to almost 10 000 separate salmon stocks. Many are small, perhaps only a few hundred fish, but all are genetically distinct.

This variability, according to Harvey, has served salmon well. The future of any species—including *Homo sapiens* — is greatly improved over the long term if it can draw on a wide range of characteristics embodied in many different stocks. This way, when a species faces a challenge such as climate change or disease, the chances are greater that one or more of its various stocks will have the innate ability to overcome the threat, allowing the species itself to survive. Without genetic diversity, species become more uniform— and more vulnerable. If only one strain of rice existed, for example, a vigorous new blight could wipe out much of the world's food supply almost overnight.

To illustrate some of the threats facing salmon today, World Fisheries Trust has developed a "salmon survival" board game called *Up the Creek*. One evening, I try it out with friends; we soon get a taste of how tough it is to be a Pacific salmon. Each player adopts a specific stock: the Bowron River sockeye, for instance, or the Kitimat River coho. You head downstream and into the ocean by rolling dice and dealing with a multitude of natural and human-created "events," most of them hazardous to your health. Each turn, you receive "survival" cards with useful features—extra food, for instance, or reduced fishing—which you may be able to use to counteract the hazards. To win the game you must avoid extinction and return to your spawning grounds with as many "health" points as possible.

The events each player faces mirror the dangers facing actual fish stocks. The most serious of these involve the destruction of freshwater habitat by human activity. Logging impacts alone include slides, erosion, sedimentation, loss of shade and organic debris, water temperature increases and herbicide poisoning. Mine effluents can be deadly to fish, too. Hydroelectric dams eliminate entire valleys, as they have on the Columbia River, where most salmon runs are now extinct.

Overfishing is a problem in many areas, especially when commercial fishers set their nets for healthy salmon runs that have been enhanced by hatcheries but end up catching rare wild stocks by mistake. Rapid urbanization, especially in southwestern B.C., is having a major effect on salmon habitat. Streams are converted to culverts and polluted by sewage, stormwater and landfill leachates. In the Fraser estuary, diking, dredging and log booming have transformed 80 percent of the wetlands where millions of juvenile salmon spend a vital part of their lives.

The perils listed so far are merely the ones we know about. Interactions between wild salmon stocks and the province's eager-to-expand aquaculture industry pose new difficulties. The farmed fish are Atlantic salmon, a different species, and escapees compete with wild Pacific salmon for food and pass on diseases and parasites. Climatic changes such as El Niño can affect salmon on a vast scale by introducing new predators and eliminating traditional food sources.

Up the Creek is entertaining, and it can remind us that, for salmon, life is not a game. A few stocks are healthy—often because of years of enhancement by hatchery programs— but many are vanishing. Some have already expired. A 1991 study in the northwest U.S. identified 106 extinct and 214 threatened salmon stocks. Three years later, the Oregon and Washington salmon fisheries shut down. A major 1996 report, which assessed only half of Canada's West Coast salmon stocks due to incomplete data, was especially alarming. It found that about 1000 runs are either extinct, at a high risk of extinction or of "special concern."

On the west coast of Vancouver Island, 75 percent of pink salmon stocks and 63 percent of chinook stocks are endangered. The Stranby River pink run near Cape Scott has declined from 16 000 fish to 50, Kyuquot Sound's Artlish River chinook run from 4000 fish to fewer than 100. The list goes on and on. Many runs were lost long before anyone had a chance to study them. Vancouver, for instance, once had fifty salmon streams; now it has two. Scientists estimate that 30 percent of the chinook stocks in the Strait of Georgia have disappeared.

Adequate genetic diversity gives salmon a fighting chance against life's vicissitudes. Over the course of thousands of years, the loss of a few stocks is not the end of the world. Some will inevitably die out anyway, and other runs will become established and take their place. But over the short term, B.C.'s salmon species cannot afford to keep losing large numbers of stocks. "What we're seeing today," says Brian Harvey, "is a piecemeal death of the resource, a slow process of attrition." We may soon reach a point of no return.

His International Fisheries Gene Bank is like one of the survival cards in *Up the Creek*: it buys society a little time to tackle the root causes of the problem. But it is no panacea. Because stocks face multiple threats, saving them will require complex solutions. Protecting spawning and rearing grounds is critical. But which habitats are a priority? Streambeds need to be restored and rivers cleaned up in such a way that biodiversity is increased. The same need applies to hatchery programs. From a genetic viewpoint, little is gained by further improving large, healthy salmon runs when so many small, weak runs are at risk. Fortunately, small-scale hatcheries and portable egg incubators are now being developed that will allow enhancement efforts to be applied to the smallest stream.

Improved commercial harvesting techniques can also contribute to stock survival, scientists believe. There is a huge difference between taking a hundred salmon from one genetic stock and taking one from each of a hundred stocks. On the dock, the results look the same, but the first fishery represents genocide while the second one may be sustainable. The accidental bycatch of threatened salmon runs can be reduced, according to Harvey. More fishing activity needs to be restricted to areas where salmon stocks are better separated. Improved fishing gear—sunken gillnets that allow shallow-swimming species to proceed; fishwheels, weirs and traps; modified trawls designed to retain only species of a certain size—can be used. And overall fishing quotas should be lowered.

To further conserve wild stocks, information must be gathered on their habits and abundance. For instance, World Fisheries Trust and the Nuu-chah-nulth Tribal Council are attempting to rebuild Vancouver Island's much depleted Clayoquot Sound sockeye fishery, using hatcheries and portable incubators. Each stock, and there are many, has to be identified if enhancement is to be effective. Fin tissue samples are clipped and DNA is "fingerprinted" to determine each stock's unique genetic signature, showing which are related and which distinct. The resulting data will enable managers to fine-tune enhancement efforts, discover which runs migrate together and, eventually, design a selective fishery that will protect the weaker stocks. This kind of aquatic research is vital, says Harvey.

Increased public awareness, he believes, is the final element needed to help save salmon, and much of his time is taken up giving lectures and media interviews and preparing educational materials—such as *Up the Creek*. The philosophy of the World Fisheries Trust is that people will support change once they understand the issues. Widespread public interest in saving salmon runs will lead to practical improvements: more careful road-building, the rehabilitation of community streams, tougher anti-pollution measures, improved fishing gear. Through our own efforts we can give our much-loved salmon species a better chance to survive.

By Way of Water

MY PERSONAL WATERCRAFT, as you've probably gathered by now, is a kayak: twenty-five kilograms of fibreglass moulded into a sleek narrow shape that I wear around my hips. I can pack enough supplies into this fragile shell to keep me alive for months if I catch fish en route. Depending on the weather and my fear level, I can paddle to almost any point on the British Columbia coast. I must admit, though, that there are more comfortable modes of travel.

A coastal way of life is a nautical way of life. It means messing around in boats or at least watching a passing parade of vessels fishing and towing and cruising. It means catching ferries and wishing you had a yacht (especially when you're camping in the rain). Over the last few years I've been fortunate to explore different parts of the coast in very different ways: on a luxurious ketch, a working freighter, a refurbished missionary boat, all sizes and shapes of ferry—and in my kayak, of course. Here are accounts of some of those trips, plus a profile of a veteran tugboat captain.

If you detect an element of nostalgia creeping into some stories, I make no apology for it. The days when you could jump on a Union steamship and head just about anywhere in the Pacific Northwest sound fine to me. Perhaps I made these journeys to relive accounts I'd read of excursions in the 1920s and '30s. But coastal cruising is on the rise again, with more ferries and tourist craft being rushed into service to meet the growing demand. We may yet see another gilded age of maritime travel along B.C.'s shores.

ISLAND ROAMER

ACROSS JUAN PEREZ SOUND on Moresby Island, the kilometre-high peaks of the San Cristoval Range are sprinkled with late-spring snow. The pale blue sky is cloudless, the air bracingly cool. And the bathwater? Well, the bathwater is hot but comfortable—and crystal clear, as well. It's early May in the Queen Charlotte Islands, and we have Hotspring Island to ourselves.

In June, the Haida Watchmen will occupy the cabins on the beach below. A steady stream of travellers will start to arrive. As we did earlier, they'll head first for the bath shed, fitted with a deep concrete tub and three moveable pipes bearing hot, warm and cool water. It's a rustic, elegant arrangement, not unlike an Asian bathhouse. Soak down, soap up, rinse off with the jug provided, empty and clean the tub, then venture out to sample three natural pools, each with different temperatures. Finally, sink into a blissful torpor, especially if you're a kayaker and you've been camping for any length of time.

We don't have that excuse, but get blissed anyway. When at last we return to the *Island Roamer*, a twenty-one-metre ketch we are more than content to call home for nine days, we fall on our lunch of lentil soup and toasted cheese muffins

With the San Cristoval Range in the background, the *Island Roamer* closes in on Moresby Island. (ANDREW SCOTT)

like people who have actually been working. There are six-teen of us altogether: twelve ecotourists and a crew of four. We are doing something I've wanted, badly, to do for over two decades: meandering along the coast of Moresby and its adjacent islands, visiting abandoned Haida village sites, old mining and whaling settlements, and biological hotspots.

The *Roamer* roams on behalf of Bluewater Adventures, owned by Randy Burke, who leads many of the expeditions. The boat visits Desolation Sound, southeast Alaska, Knight Inlet and other areas, but the Charlottes—or Haida Gwaii, as the Haida people call their 150-island homeland—is its specialty. We meet Burke briefly, after flying from Sandspit, site of the islands' main airport, to Poole Inlet, 110 kilome-tres south, where the *Roamer* awaits us. The single-engine Otter follows Moresby's rugged rocky spine, and despite the copious clearcuts, the flight provides a fine overview of Gwaii Haanas National Park Reserve, which covers the southern third of the archipelago and is inaccessible by road. It's here we'll be spending most of our time.

Burke greets us, then joins the returning tour group for the trip back to Sandspit. We are now at the mercy of skipper Peter Heiberg, a sardonic Englishman whose dry wit and hilarious one-liners keep us in stitches for much of the journey. Helping Heiberg are Linda Nichol, a biologist and marine-mammal specialist from Victoria; Iain Jones, a cheerful college student from Coquitlam who is serving as assistant naturalist, deckhand and, should the need arise, plumber; and Pat Murray, our indefatigable cook, who flew down with us. With only a couple of hours to prepare, here's what Murray serves for dinner that first night: coho salmon stuffed with crabmeat, shrimp and water chestnuts; fresh asparagus; new potatoes; salad; and ice cream with fresh strawberries for dessert. All hail the cook.

The sixteen-year-old *Island Roamer* is perfect for this type of cruising. With eight double-occupancy guest cabins aft of the large, book-lined lounge, and crew quarters forward, the boat can comfortably accommodate twenty people. The three heads are equipped with hot showers, and several of the cabins have double-width berths. There's plenty of seating on deck in the covered wheelhouse, where tables fold down for *al fresco* dining, and in an open area behind it. The *Roamer* is large enough for comfort and privacy, small enough for getting to know the crew and other passengers.

No two itineraries are identical. Each journey is subject to weather, tide, season and the preferences of those aboard. There are, of course, regional highlights no one wants to miss, and everyone hopes to see whales and bears and other wild creatures. Some groups are keen to go sailing. Others wish to spend plenty of time ashore exploring the natural world or island history or the vigorous, artistic realm of the Haida.

Frequent jaunts in the *Roamer*'s two outboard-equipped rubber inflatables help keep the schedule flexible. Paddlers have access to a pair of two-person plastic kayaks.

Each day we float through a different fragment of paradise. We skirt the myriad islets and channels that make up Moresby's eastern shoreline, admiring the intense, moody landscape and its green mantle of old growth: Sitka spruce, hemlock, cedar. Bald eagles wheel round us, and seabirds—auklets, murrelets, storm petrels, guillemots—ride the ocean waves and dive beneath the surface in search of prey. The tourist season has yet to begin, and we rarely see another vessel.

At regular intervals, Heiberg divides us in half—"top half or bottom half," he jokes; "it doesn't really matter"—to form shore parties, and we zoom off in the inflatables. A walk on tiny Slug Island takes us through a lush jungle of paintbrush, sea-watch and black lily. Vivid yellow blossoms of cinquefoil and stonecrop decorate the rocks. Next day we clamber up a streambed at Bag Harbour, zigzagging round huge red-cedar roots. Moss carpets nearly every visible surface; giant beards of lichen hang from the branches. On the forest floor we find dozens of little heaps of bone—fin fragments, jaws and a spine—where spawned-out salmon have provided meals for fortunate island residents and fertilized the surrounding soil.

In De La Bêche Inlet, we go ashore and slog up a hillside in the rain to view one of Haida Gwaii's semi-vertical "bonsai" bogs. In a bed of sphagnum moss, stunted cedars and gnarled lodgepole pines struggle to grow. Labrador tea and salal flourish, and such unusual plants as bog laurels and shooting stars are flowering. Despite the damp, many of us end up exploring the peat on our knees, much to the mock exasperation of the skipper. "We'll be a little late," Heiberg radioes back to the boat, rolling his eyes. "They've found another flower." When we return, slightly bedraggled, Murray restores our spirits with a dinner of roast pork in green peppercorn sauce, turnip and apple purée and raspberry cake.

By late afternoon we are usually anchored in some protected cove or inlet. Then Katherine and I often break out one of the kayaks and drift off for a more intimate encounter with Gwaii Haanas, the "place of wonder." In Louscoone Inlet we peer over the side at moon snails and opalescent ringed top shells, at orange-tentacled sea cucumbers and electric-pink sea slugs. A family of raccoons turns over rocks a short distance away. An early morning paddle through the Bischoff Islands reveals white plumose anemones, red rock crabs, miniature sharp-nosed kelp crabs and many different algaes with exotic names, such as sea brush and Turkish towel. In Ikeda Cove, site of an old copper mine and Japanese graveyard, we drift along for twenty minutes watching one of the Queen Charlottes' gigantic black bears patrol the shore.

We also paddle from the *Island Roamer* to the beach at Tanu, arriving at this former village roughly the same way the Haida people did centuries ago. Tanu, for me, has a dark, melancholy presence. It is being swallowed up by the forest. Trees have grown around house pits and along the beach; spruce roots engulf ancient posts and beams. Everything is eroded, decaying, mossy, collapsed. A few designs can still be deciphered on the undersides of fallen memorial and mortuary poles, especially near the largest pit, where the big house of Klue, an important Haida chief, once stood. At the far end of the village, broken gravestones commemorate a tragedy: a mass burial during one of the nineteenth-century smallpox epidemics that doomed Tanu.

Another day we go ashore at Skedans, a forsaken village on Louise Island, situated on an exposed isthmus between two beaches. There are several standing and leaning poles there, some with identifiable killer whale and raven crests, others with the unadorned cylindrical markings that denote the number of potlatches a particular chief had given. Each house at Skedans once had a distinctive name: Easy-to-enter, Something-terrible-happened, Dressed-up-to-show-off-all-the-time, Grizzly-bear's-mouth. Now all that's left are depressions in the wind-scoured grass.

The waters off the east coast of Moresby Island are mostly calm and protected. On occasion, however, the wind freshens. Sometimes it picks up at the same time that we need to head out into Hecate Strait in order to skirt some point or headland. Then the crew straps everything down, and we go on an exhilarating roller-coaster ride. The *Roamer* is a seaworthy craft and proves a surprisingly stable platform in the heavy swells. We don't do much sailing on this tour, but one breezy afternoon we help Heiberg and Jones get the main and mizzen sails up, and they teach us, among other things, the difference between a sheet and a halyard.

Linda Nichol, our naturalist, keeps a sharp eye out for marine mammals. She has raised expectations with after-dinner slide shows about whales and whaling, but we've seen no cetaceans in their natural glory—only dozens of Steller sea lions basking on the rookery at Garcin Rocks. Nichol regularly throws a hydrophone over the side in hopes of hearing whale messages, but all we ever get is ocean static. "Sounds like the urinals at the Yale Hotel at closing time," says Heiberg, referring to a popular Vancouver watering hole.

Our luck changes in Skidegate Inlet, where we spot a spouting grey whale, which turns out to be four grey whales feeding in shallow water. We watch them for an hour, eating our lunch on deck as they stir up theirs on the muddy sea floor. They dive over and over again, flashing their mottled grey and white tails and backs, until the water is brown with silt.

Despite forty years on the B.C. coast, this is the first time I've seen grey whales. I'm amazed at how undisturbed they are by our presence. Sixty years ago, commercial whaling was big business in the Charlottes. The other day we'd passed the inappropriately named Rose Harbour, where thousands of sperm, humpback and fin whales were reduced to barrels of oil between 1910 and 1943. The harbour is one of the last pieces of privately owned land in Gwaii Haanas. Its handful of holdout residents, who live amid the rusting debris of the old rendering plant, have ferociously resisted all attempts by Parks Canada to remove them.

Neither the whales nor Gwaii Haanas can be taken for granted. The park's spectacular 147 000-hectare wilderness, which is slowly attracting more and more visitors from around the world (1800 in 1998), was only preserved in 1987, after roadblocks and arrests and decades of protest over logging practices. Today the reserve is co-managed by the federal government and the Haida Nation. Strict regulations protect the delicate environment, and Haida Watchmen are based at the most popular destinations in the summer months. All travellers must have permits to enter, and no more than twelve people are allowed at any one spot at one time.

These rules make particular sense at Anthony Island, near the southern edge of the park, where the UNESCO World Heritage Site of Skun'gwaii, sometimes known as Ninstints, is on every visitor's itinerary. Here can be found the last large assembly of Haida poles in their original location. An uncontrolled tourist influx could easily destroy this unique, fragile place.

As we near Skun'gwaii, an auspicious omen: flocks of rhinoceros auklets, flying and swimming. Their peculiar white moustaches and eye plumes are plain against the dark water, as are the pronounced yellow horns on their beaks. Then we spot the auklets' even more bizarre cousin, the tufted puffin. With its great orange bill and golden ear tufts, this species appears almost comical: a jester in the court of birds.

As I go below to prepare for Skun'gwaii, the *Roamer* is rocking to and fro and a strong whiff of diesel hits me. Instant nausea. Wonderful, I think. Here we are at the climax of the trip and I'm sick. I struggle ashore where, if anything, I feel worse. As we hike into one of B.C.'s holiest and most mystical settings, my main and urgent concern is to find the new $30 000 chemical toilet. But it's not operational, so I settle for a $30 toilet instead. Finally, I enter Skun'gwaii a new man, shaking, purged, fully receptive to its intense spiritual charge.

Again, we have the site to ourselves. After a brief shower, the sun comes out. From the forest floats the haunting, flutelike song of the hermit thrush. The village sits on a calm cove beside a pretty pebble beach, where huge dugout canoes once rested. The open ocean is just a few metres away. Many poles are quite well preserved, some carved with the faces of eagle and raven, dogfish and bear. On one, a mossy frog crawls under the fluke of a killer whale. Notched posts and gables half-stand in the house pits.

Skun'gwaii has an atmosphere of total serenity. Gradually, each one of us falls silent. We wander in awe, then find private spots to commune with the spirits of this place. To me, they seem welcoming. As I sit and contemplate, I swear I can hear the laughter of children, beckoning me, inviting me to draw in Haida Gwaii's healing energy and transform myself.

NANAIMO TILLICUM

IN CAPTAIN BILL THOMPSON's scrapbook, a photograph from the front page of the *Vancouver Daily Province* catches the eye. Four rugged-looking men, two with cigarettes dangling nonchalantly from their lips, are smiling at each other—with relief, perhaps. "Safe and Sound after Ordeal," reads the headline. The clipping, dated December 22, 1951, describes how the tug *Caterpillar Chief* sank in icy waters off Bowen Island in Howe Sound.

"It all happened so suddenly," the tug's skipper says in the article. "I was at the wheel and all at once I felt her list to the side. I looked out the rear door and saw that the galley and stern were awash. We all scurried into the lifeboat and it seemed like just a minute before she sank."

Bill Thompson, the skipper in question, was twenty-five at the time. Today, forty-eight years later, he's sitting in the snug wheelhouse of another tug, the *Nanaimo Tillicum*, as he tells me the story. He still doesn't know exactly how it happened. A hatch may have come loose in heavy seas. "Some newspaper reporters asked me why the *Chief* went down, and I told them 'excessive moisture in the engine-room,' and they printed that," he says with a laugh. When you've spent most of a lifetime in the marine towing

Captain Bill
Thompson welcomes
visitors aboard the
Nanaimo Tillicum.
(Courtesy
Thompson Family)

business, mystery and danger go along with the job.

Thompson has been saviour as well as saved. His was the first boat on the scene when the big wooden steam tug *Commodore Straits* struck Fraser Rock in Welcome Passage north of Sechelt. This was in 1955, also in December, and Thompson was captain of a tug called the *Nanaimo Clipper* at the time. He'd just got married and his wife happened to be with him on the boat. "The *Straits* was sitting up on the rock," he recalls, "bow way out, stern half underwater, steam coming out all over the place." He put his bow up against her, and the crew of ten scrambled aboard. "Then I backed off and down she went." Thompson remembers that his wife's eyes were bulging out so far, "you could have knocked them off with a stick." Later, he assisted in a salvage attempt on the tug, but it broke loose during the operation and was written off. Today, the *Commodore Straits* is a popular dive site.

As a deckhand for Nanaimo Towing in 1948, Thompson was paid $125 and got three days off each month. "That was not too bad in those days," he reflects. Accommodation was spartan. "A boat this size," he says, indicating the eighteen-metre, thirty-two-tonne *Tillicum*, "would have five guys stacked in the bow like cordwood. As long as you could find a place to sleep, you were happy." In 1960, by which time he had moved to Pender Harbour on the Sunshine Coast and Straits Towing had acquired Nanaimo Towing, he decided to go into business for himself.

Thompson made a deal with Straits to buy the *Nanaimo Tillicum* and do the company's yarding work in Jervis and Sechelt inlets, making up log booms for larger tugs to lug to Howe Sound. "We would come up to the camps and get the logs," he explains, "and take them across the channel from Earls Cove. Straits had a tie-up spot there. Log towing is a lot safer since they went to bundle booms, which take more weather than the flat booms. With a fifteen- to twenty-mile-per-hour wind, flat booms start to lose logs. And the owners of those logs don't like that."

Thompson named his own company Tillicum Towing. Today his sons Garry and Pat run the show. Tillicum owns a number of boats and scows, including a small freighter named the *Klassen*, which was purchased from the government after being confiscated in a drug bust, a powered barge called the *Bad News* and two more tugs: the *Genni Bay* and the *Glen Roamer*. The Thompsons specialize in running feed to B.C.'s fish farms, taking 2000 tonnes of meal from Vancouver each trip on a five-day voyage through Georgia and Johnstone straits to northern Vancouver Island, offloading at sixty-two different aquaculture establishments.

You could say that Bill Thompson's life is totally wrapped up with tugs. But that wouldn't be quite true. It's wrapped up with planes, as well, and cars, and family members, many of whom live along the same stretch of Hospital Bay shoreline that he and his wife, Wilma, occupy. When I arrive at their home for the first time, Thompson is changing the oil in an immaculate Model A Ford. Airplane parts, including several wing frames, are sprinkled generously around the property. Down at the dock, a red Cessna 180 floatplane is moored next to the *Tillicum*. Both boat and captain are pretty well retired now from the towing trade. ("I still work the same hours," he claims. "I just don't get paid any more.")

The most amazing craft—one I've stopped to admire on previous jaunts round Pender Harbour—is parked on an adjacent float. It's a canary yellow U.S. Navy N3N-3 biplane that Thompson has restored to perfect working order. In fact, he is planning to taxi out into the harbour and take it for a spin this very evening. "Most people who like boats also like airplanes," he says offhandedly, as if having a gleaming World War II trainer in your backyard is nothing unusual. "There isn't a hell of a lot of difference between flying and boating. That biplane there is really a sailboat. Same principle."

Twenty-five years ago, Thompson helped found the Canadian Museum of Flight, now located in Langley. Besides rebuilding his own planes, he has also helped salvage planes for the museum, including a World War II Hampden bomber that crashed near Victoria and was retrieved from a depth of 200 metres. Salvage work is always a challenge, says Thompson, which makes it particularly enjoyable. He's a licensed pilot, of course, as are two of his four sons and his daughter. Did I mention that he's also a certified diver?

We're here today to talk tugs, however, so we settle down in the shipshape, wood-panelled cabin of the *Nanaimo Tillicum*, where a microwave oven and an industrial-strength depth finder contrast with the brassy gleam of the binnacle and ship's wheel. Built in 1924 for a Vancouver piledriving outfit and originally named the *Dan King*, the tug is two years older than its present owner. Its first engine was enormous: a direct-reversing Atlas, four metres long and six tonnes in weight, that put out all of 135 horsepower. When Thompson decided to retire the *Tillicum* and make it into a pleasure boat, he put in a slow but economical engine, a 152-horsepower Gardner. He made other changes, too, rebuilding the cabin and making it more spacious and comfortable for cruising, and updating the head and the galley. "I wanted the boat to look the same from the side, though," he says, "so I didn't change the profile."

For their first recreational trip, Bill and Wilma took the *Nanaimo Tillicum* to Alaska. But for scenery, he declares, "there's nothing in Alaska that there isn't in B.C. Instead of taking big trips, I'd rather go for a week at a time." He's just back, for instance, from doing a little fishing off the north end of Vancouver Island. And he and Wilma love to go to gatherings organized by the International Retired Tugboat Association, where West Coast tugs of all ages and descriptions get together for jolly weekends.

The little town of Gibsons on Howe Sound hosted one such rendezvous in July of 1999. Three thousand people thronged the public wharf, which was lined with a marvellous collection of towboats—nineteen in all. There was the *Elmore* from Seattle, built in 1890; the luxurious, thirty-eight-metre *Yellowfin* from Orcas Island; the *Forest Surveyor*, a cozy liveaboard and former B.C. Forest Service tug; the 1922 *Master*, complete with operational steam engine. Some tugs, such as the twenty-eight-metre *Sea Wave* from Vancouver, while no longer towing, were still working hard for the charter trade. The freshly painted *Glendevon*, by contrast, partway through a rebuild that had already cost a reported $1 million and not even touched the interior yet, looked too clean for work. And then, of course, there was the *Nanaimo Tillicum*.

"They treated us good at Gibsons," says Thompson. His favourite tug bash, though, is held each Labour Day weekend at Olympia, Washington, where thirty-five to forty tugs show up for races, an open house and some pretty intense socializing. "They turn the docks right over to us. It's a real festival, with booth after booth of people selling stuff. We never miss it."

Of course, most of the skippers in the retired tugboat association are not true towboat men, Thompson notes. "They're frustrated towboat men. They're veterinarians and lawyers and whatever who have always wanted to go to sea. Now they've got the chance. They are captains in name only, but they're sure enjoying themselves."

DOGWOOD PRINCESS II

AT LANGDALE TERMINAL on the west shore of Howe Sound, the passenger-only *Dogwood Princess II* looks like a nursling berthed beside the *Queen of Surrey*. But they are sister ships. As we walk down the ramp to board the *Princess* early one morning, I have to remind myself that BC Ferries' smallest vessel is not a toy. In the same way that the gigantic *Queen* towering above us serves as a lifeline for thousands of people living on B.C.'s Sunshine Coast, the *Princess* also maintains vital, year-round links in the province's marine highway system.

Ten times a day—more often on Fridays, weekends and holidays—the *Princess* neatly skirts the *Queen*'s massive stern and speeds away to the offlying communities of New Brighton on Gambier Island, and Eastbourne and Keats Landing on Keats Island. Keats and Gambier are Howe Sound's "other" main islands. They aren't as well known or as heavily populated as Bowen Island, which is served by ferry from Horseshoe Bay and has become almost a bedroom suburb of Vancouver. Keats and Gambier are inhabited year-round by a small number of determined homesteaders and can get busy in summer. Still, they are rustic in comparison to Bowen or most of the Gulf Islands. Exploring them is a pleasant way to spend a sunny day.

B.C.'s smallest ferry runs between Langdale and Gambier and Keats islands in Howe Sound. (ANDREW SCOTT)

Rob Bennie spends four days out of every eight plying these waters. He is one of the *Dogwood Princess*'s two skippers, and he has worked on Howe Sound for twenty-five years. The shifts are long—the ferry operates from 7:30 a.m. to 6:40 p.m. (7:15 p.m. on Fridays), and even later if an extra trip is necessary, as happens from time to time on Sundays— but the two-man crews get used to them. Bennie, who grew up just down the road from the terminal at Hopkins Landing, wouldn't have any other life. "I'm my own boss," he says. "This run is a lot more personal than the others, where you may be packing anywhere from 300 to over a thousand people. We get to know everyone on the islands. I think it's one of the best jobs in the fleet."

The *Princess* was built at Sidney on Vancouver Island in 1979, and custom designed for the Howe Sound service.

She's a water-taxi, really—thirteen metres long, twenty-one tonnes in weight—with a large enclosed cabin for thirty-eight passengers and a functional, no-nonsense layout. The power plant has been upgraded over the years; twin Volvo diesels are currently capable of moving her at a twenty-one-knot (forty-kilometre-per-hour) maximum, though her usual cruising speed is slightly less than that.

Howe Sound's first ferry, an unnamed sailboat that operated in the late 1880s, was somewhat slower. So were its successors: the *Saturna*, the *Britannia* and several Union steamships, among other craft. Tymac and Sea Bus water taxis shuttled passengers from Gibsons Landing and Horseshoe Bay in the 1940s. Mercury Launch and Tug Ltd. still offers year-round Friday and weekend service from Horseshoe Bay to Eastbourne on Keats and half a dozen ports on Gambier. They can also arrange freight and vehicle transport.

Gambier boasts approximately one hundred full-time residents, Keats only thirty to forty. The population of each island jumps to around 400 in summer. Fifteen youngsters commute to Langdale on weekdays and travel by bus to Gibsons to attend school. *Dogwood Princess* passengers can only take on board what they can carry, which means that plenty of shopping bags are usually in evidence. The sign at the dock advises that explosives, bicycles and livestock are forbidden, but dogs are another matter. Islanders love dogs, especially golden Labs, and I've yet to travel on the *Princess* without a couple of furry footwarmers blocking the aisle.

Journeys are short. To cross Thornbrough Channel from Langdale to New Brighton on Gambier takes all of ten minutes. Today, midweek in April, about a dozen passengers are making the trip. They disperse to a row of worn vehicles after we arrive and quickly disappear. My partner and I spend the morning tramping a network of dirt roads connecting

New Brighton to docks at West Bay and Gambier Harbour.
At the island's southwest tip, grassy tracks lead to secluded
Avalon Bay. Elsewhere, hikers can make a five-hour trek to
a lake nestled between two of Gambier's peaks. We decide,
instead, to stop for an excellent homemade lunch at the tiny
heritage Gambier Island General Store.

Gambier's thick forests have long attracted loggers, and
the island was the site of an early Howe Sound sawmill. By
the 1920s, several settlers had built substantial farms on the
south shore. The island is also rich in minerals. In the 1970s
a huge open-pit copper-molybdenum mine was proposed that
would cover two-thirds of Gambier, set off dynamite day
and night and require an industrial port. Residents fought
a bitter, five-year battle against the project, eventually
forcing the mineral company to abandon its plans.

Although Gambier is the largest island in Howe Sound,
its road system is far less developed than Bowen's. The
interior is wild and mountainous. On the south shore, two
flanking headlands stretch towards the Strait of Georgia like
the paws of a giant forest-covered sphinx. In their grasp are
three deep bays, all major log-booming grounds in their day.
Long Bay, or Port Graves, I remember from childhood summers spent at Artaban, an Anglican camp. Centre Bay is the
site of several yacht club outstations. At Gambier's southeast corner, Halkett Bay Provincial Marine Park beckons
boaters and paddlers.

We rejoin the *Princess* for the trip to Eastbourne, on the
side of Keats closest to Vancouver. This passage takes the
vessel out into the middle of the sound and down
Collingwood Channel, where she can be exposed to wintry
weather. "We've had some good storms here," says Bennie,
who recalls making the run with a fearsome northerly or
"Squamish" wind blasting sixty-knot (110-kilometre-per-hour)

gusts of freezing spray against his wheelhouse. He only remembers one trip ever being cancelled, though.

The jaunt over to Keats Island is not much longer than the one to Gambier. At Eastbourne dock, a single person disembarks. No one gets on. Now we are the boat's only passengers. We don't explore Eastbourne on this trip, though one could easily walk the four-kilometre unpaved road that links the dock to Keats Landing, then reboard the *Princess* for the run back to Langdale. Eastbourne, like many Howe Sound settlements, started life as a summer camp. Harry White and other early homesteaders sold land there to the United and Presbyterian churches, which ran camps in the 1930s and '40s. Later, a distinct community evolved, with at least 150 cottages. Some are quite elegant, and one, the Old Lodge, is supposedly haunted. Dating from the 1920s, the Old Lodge has been a general store, post office, private home and bed and breakfast. Today it's a rental property. Several guests claim to have seen a ghost there and heard disembodied voices.

The journey from Eastbourne to Keats Landing offers Rob Bennie a choice of two routes. The inner passage, north to Cotton Point and then west round Observatory Point, is more protected and slightly shorter, and that's the one he usually takes. En route, the *Princess* passes the site of the old Corkum Farm, a Howe Sound landmark familiar to anyone who has taken the ferry between Langdale and Horseshoe Bay. Today, the farm is managed and partly owned by the Barnabas Family Ministries. Non-denominational conferences and retreats are held in the renovated farmhouse and a new, twelve-room lodge.

With only two passengers aboard, and curious ones at that, Bennie opts this afternoon for the southerly route from Eastbourne to the landing. This alternative takes the *Princess* down Barfleur Passage right to the mouth of Howe Sound. To the east, we can almost see into the vacation homes on the pretty little islands of the Pasley Group. As we cruise along, Bennie tells us about another highlight of his job: wildlife watching. Almost every day he sees seals and sea lions and all kinds of birds, including bald eagles plucking fish from the waves. He exited Langdale a few years ago just as a pod of killer whales was passing by; a cow and her calf swam right across his bow.

In summer, when the cottagers arrive and the church camps really get going, Howe Sound can become thick with boats, some as reckless as the killer whale pair. The *Princess* has never been involved in an accident, though she has been called upon to put out boat and cottage fires and to attend the odd medical emergency in the middle of the night.

As Bennie eases his vessel round Home Island off the southern tip of Keats and enters Shoal Channel to the west of the island, the town of Gibsons comes into view. Directly opposite is the dock at Keats Landing, with the wide grassy clearings of the Baptist camp on the gentle slope behind. John Hooper, one of the island's first homesteaders, settled here in 1888. He sold his property to Henry Brown around 1905, and Brown, with the help of hired Japanese labour, turned it into a thriving estate. Rocks were cleared and made into low walls. A water reservoir was built. Hectares of orchard and garden eventually flourished.

This interlude ended in 1920, when fire destroyed Brown's farmhouse. Six years later, the land was sold for a summer camp to the Convention of Baptist Churches of British Columbia. To raise the necessary capital, a group of Baptist businessmen formed Keats Island Summer Homes Ltd. and sold shares and 99-year leases for cottage lots to Baptist families. Leaseholders agreed to maintain an interest in the camp, not use alcohol and give the company right of first refusal if they wanted to sell. Soon dozens of simple cottages surrounded the central campgrounds. Over the years, many leases changed hands through sale or inheritance. As a result, some of today's seventy-odd cottage owners are not Baptists and have little interest in the camp, and that has been the cause of problems and strained relationships. But many cottages have also passed down in Baptist families, and a strong cooperative bond still exists between Keats Camps, which continues to offer popular summer programs, and the bulk of the cottagers.

At Keats Landing, Bennie picks up a passenger and zips over to Gibsons harbour for fuel. This is where the passenger was headed anyway, so he jumps ship at Gibsons while we stay aboard for the return run to Langdale. On the way we pass the privately owned Shelter Islets and Plumper Cove, site of a popular provincial marine park. Past influences can be felt here, too. The islets were once a Squamish First Nation reserve and reputed burial site. Plumper Cove bordered the pioneer McDonald farm.

As we head home, our skipper reflects on the future. The Howe Sound service will undoubtedly change over the coming years, as it has, often, in the past. "We make our own schedule here," says Bennie, "adjusting it to local travel patterns in consultation with the islanders." Urban recreationists, he points out, are gradually discovering Howe Sound. More and more summer places are being built. More and more passengers are using the ferry service. They're wanting to bring bulkier goods with them, such as bicycles and small freight items. When the *Dogwood Princess* reaches the end of her working life over the next few years, a larger vessel would make sense on the run. But, ironically, the islanders may end up with a smaller one.

The Howe Sound routes lose $300 000 a year, and the ferry corporation originally wanted to privatize the service. But the islanders, fearing an increase in the modest $3.75 adult fare, didn't like the idea, and it was deep-sixed after the ferry workers' union vowed to fight it. The next plan called for a new, scaled-back boat that could operate with one crew member in low-demand periods and make some runs only if riders phoned ahead. Ferry brass figured these changes might cut the operating deficit in half. Islanders weren't crazy about this scheme, either, which is now in limbo anyway, as it doesn't meet Coast Guard regulations. The present service, it seems, will last a little longer. My advice? Enjoy a ride on the *Princess* while you can.

COLUMBIA III

CURIOUS TO HEAR what one of my fellow travellers has captured with his sensitive little digital audiotape recorder, I slide the earphones into place and switch the machine on. Instantly, I'm transported back to the lost world of Mamalilaculla, an abandoned First Nations village on the central B.C. coast that we'd visited earlier that day. Crows complain; waves slap lazily against the beach; bees rhapsodize over blossoms of honeysuckle, cherry and lilac. A sudden whirring sound swerves from speaker to speaker: rufous hummingbirds, drunk on nectar. Eventually, rain plocks on the big thimbleberry leaves, adding its voice to the chorus.

Though we had paddled to Mamalilaculla on Village Island—six of us in four kayaks—we are now safely returned to our mothership, the *M.V. Columbia III*, a twenty-one-metre former Anglican mission boat. We'll spend the night here in Potts Bay on Midsummer Island, 340 kilometres northwest of Victoria, protected from the wind rising off nearby Queen Charlotte Strait. And over dinner—Greek salad, smoked-salmon pasta and glasses of Captain Bill's homemade pinot noir—we'll marvel at what we've seen.

The *Columbia*, beautifully refurbished with an eye to transporting kayaks and kayakers along the B.C. coast, can

The *Columbia*'s latest incarnation is as a "mothership" for lucky kayakers.
(ANDREW SCOTT)

sleep ten, but we are only seven. When we'd joined the
boat at Port McNeill on northern Vancouver Island, owner
and skipper Bill McKechnie asked us what we hoped to do.
Paddling, of course, is high on our list of priorities, as is
learning more about the culture of the region's first inhabitants, the Kwakwaka'wakw. Naturally, we want to see
whales and other wild creatures. And simply hanging out
on the boat sounds good, as well.

The *Columbia* is a treasure of gleaming brass and rich
hardwoods, built in 1956 for the Columbia Coast Mission,
before aluminum and fibreglass became the norm. Operating
out of the Anglican hospital at Alert Bay, she became a well-
known, welcome sight at remote logging camps, canneries,
lighthouses and First Nations settlements. She usually carried
a crew of five: captain, chaplain, doctor, nurse and cook/
deckhand. The chaplain performed baptisms, marriages and
Sunday services in the tiny chapel, which held an altar

and portable organ and seated twenty. A short film was customarily screened after the service as an inducement to attend. Medical emergencies often required the hasty transport of some unlucky soul to the hospital. The *Columbia* was retired in the late 1970s, when floatplanes took over the job of linking coastal communities with the wider world.

A morning at Alert Bay village, the *Columbia*'s old home base and the centre of the Kwakwaka'wakw universe, gives us a feel for the region. A fabled collection of ceremonial masks and regalia, confiscated by the federal government in 1921 and returned in part in 1980, is now sheltered there in the U'mista Cultural Centre. The entrance to this fine small museum repeats an ancient log post-and-beam longhouse motif. Inside is a crowded assembly of carved, fantastic faces: bears, eagles, whales, ravens with enormous beaks that open and close, inventive masks with parts that move to reveal other masks. They last came alive at winter potlatch festivals of dancing, feasting and gift-giving, outlawed in the late nineteenth century by Canadian authorities who considered the ceremonies wasteful and profligate.

One entire wall of the museum is covered with large-scale maps. Historic villages are marked, described and illustrated with archival photographs. We would be passing some of these sites, and we gaze at the wall with curiosity. Most of the names—Cheslakee, Gwayasdums, Aglakumna, Dakiulis—are unfamiliar to me. I know a few, such as Mamalilaculla and Karlukwees, from the woodcuts of Canadian artist Walter J. Phillips. Quaee, or Kingcome, the most isolated Kwakwaka'wakw community of all, is the setting for Margaret Craven's best-selling book, *I Heard the Owl Call My Name.*

The next day, as we paddle up Village Channel through West Pass, potlatches are on my mind. The day is cloudy and calm, the only sign of civilization a distant fish farm. Small, exquisite islands, one with a masklike pictograph in red on a rock bluff, fall astern as we drift along. Those invited to Dan Cranmer's 1921 potlatch, reputedly the largest ever held on the coast, would have come this way. The celebration lasted six days. Boats, pool tables and sewing machines were given away, plus gramophones, blankets, flour and cash. Afterwards, officials arrested thirty or so participants—the first time the law against potlatching had been enforced on such a scale. Some attendees cut an infamous deal with the Crown, surrendering their dance regalia—the same artifacts we'd seen at Alert Bay—in return for suspended sentences. Others, including several older women who resisted this attempt to stamp out their way of life, were sent to jail.

The potlatch guests, like us, were headed to Mamalilaculla. The winter village sites of B.C.'s coastal First Nations were always well chosen: accessible, defensible, glorious. Mamalilaculla is no exception. As its low shoreline, protected by a shallow, islet-strewn bay, comes into view, we see deserted, Victorian-style homes, their window sockets gaping against a background of intense vegetation. Floating closer still, we catch glimpses of former glory: a massive longhouse frame. Four corner posts, bushes growing from their tops, remain, as do two arches. The outer surfaces of the logs, each well over one metre in diameter, are delicately finished, with fluted markings.

The village site is off-limits to the general public. Signs are posted on the beach. We have permission to visit, so we go ashore and wander carefully about, breathing in the heady bouquet of the flowers. A young black bear that has been gorging on berries shoots into the woods with a crash of branches. Old fallen poles, eaten away by fungi and lichen, have almost disintegrated into the wet earth. On one I can still see an image of the bear's ancestor, its ursine teeth unmistakeable; small human faces are incised into its paws. Soon little will distinguish Mamalilaculla from the forest.

Rain is plocking on the thimbleberries in earnest now. We cast a last look over the peaceful scene and leave. The sea is dead calm. Fat droplets splash on the surface of the water, creating a sheen of silver. As we kayak through the liquid mist, warm and dry under our waterproof shells, the effect is mesmerizing. In a nearby bay the *Columbia* awaits with tea, hot showers and, eventually, dinner and cozy berths.

Travelling in this manner is pure heaven for novice or nervous kayakers, and a welcome change for experienced paddlers, too, who get a break from camping in the rain. In one week on the *Columbia*, we see more countryside than we could have covered in months of traditional expedition kayaking. Sharon Comeau, the paddling instructor and guide, makes sure everyone is properly equipped, teamed with an appropriate partner and given basic technique and safety lessons. The stable, plastic, two-person kayaks are stored on the roof of the cabin and winched over the side each morning in some fabulous new location.

McKechnie, a former Victoria hotelier, has spent a small fortune fixing the *Columbia* up. He converted the old infirmary, with its dental chair and x-ray machine, to extra sleeping quarters and transformed the main cabin into a comfortable dining and lounging space, lined with books and guarded by Mao, a Tonkinese cat. The navigation and safety systems are state of the art. McKechnie and Comeau join forces to handle the cooking chores in the tiny, modern galley and turn out three delicious meals a day.

The *Columbia*'s playground is the east end of Queen Charlotte Strait, where hundreds of small islands provide protection and plenty of grand wilderness scenery. We meet many locals on our travels. At Freshwater Bay, artist Georganna Malloff welcomes kayakers to camp on her beach for a modest fee and view her unusual outdoor sculpture gallery. At Echo Bay, Jim and Christine O'Donnell offer moorage, showers, artworks and home-baked pastries to passing powerboats. One day we kayak from Growler Cove on Cracroft Island, across Blackney Passage to Hanson Island, where we get a chance to visit Orcalab and talk to the legendary Paul Spong, who has spent much of his life studying and trying to protect killer whales. At Shawl Bay, we pull up to a small dock and take on fresh water, leaving money in an honour box and laughing at the "No Boat Washing, No Laundering" sign.

Our furthest destination is remote Kingcome Inlet. We cruise for hours past a landscape of thick forest without seeing another vessel or any sign of human habitation. The water is silty with runoff; tree stumps and wood debris float everywhere. Two-thousand-metre peaks line our route, and spectacular braided waterfalls loop down sheer granite flanks. At the head of Kingcome, where a grey glacial river fans out through an estuary of mud and grass, we tie up to a log boom. This broad waterway is too shallow for the *Columbia*. From here on we'll be paddling.

Our first stop is the Halliday Ranch, abandoned only ten years ago. Three generations of Hallidays tended the Kingcome estuary, diking and draining the rich alluvial deposits, creating gorgeous meadows to graze cattle and grow hay. Now the fields are reverting to semi-swamp, and native plants are taking over again. We search out the old homestead, covered in a jungle of elderberry trees. The gardens have gone wild—hydrangeas and raspberries everywhere. Old trucks and farm gear decay steadily in the collapsing barns.

We head further upriver, working hard against the current. The banks are bordered with huge alders. I feel hemmed in by this silent world of inpenetrable green, which the welcome cry of the kingfisher finally cracks. At last, round a bend we arrive at Kingcome village. To visit a deserted village is one thing—a bit eerie, perhaps (there are ghosts at Mamalilaculla, for sure), but basically safe enough. To enter a living one is something else. Quaee, surrounded by mountains and hidden up an obscure inlet, is at the end of the world for a reason. Those who live here like their privacy. Walking along the main street, complete with ancient, decaying totem poles, is like walking, unbidden, through someone's living room.

We are here with a purpose, however—to visit Flora Dawson, a tribal elder and council member McKechnie knows. A worldly soul who was born on Village Island and has travelled to Holland and New Zealand on cultural exchanges, she greets us warmly. We meet her husband, Dave, who states cheerfully that he is fading away now that he's in his eighties, and will soon be gone. After talking a while, we leave and cross a grassy common in the centre of the village to look at the old church. Beside it stands a freshly painted thunderbird pole.

The return paddle, downstream all the way, is a breeze. On our slow journey back to Port McNeill, we patrol Blackfish Sound and Johnstone Strait, where an entire seg-ment of B.C.'s tourism industry seems dependent upon the annual return to the area of killer whales. Dozens of boats and businesses follow their every movement. Shoreline spot-ters direct orca-watching tours to the best locations. Thousands of kayaks put in every year at nearby Telegraph Cove, all of them hoping to see the big mammals.

We see killer whales as well, from the deck of the mother-ship. But my partner and I also share a more intimate thrill one day as we're paddling last in line in Trainer Passage near Eden Island. A sharp exhalation of breath behind our kayak causes us to turn quickly. Fear and fascination hold us frozen in midstroke as a colossal black body knifes momentarily through the water a short distance away. We don't see the whale again. In fact, we can't even be sure what species it is. But being that close and that vulnerable to the power of nature etches an indelible mark on our psyches. It is the kind of experience that travel on the *Columbia* seems to serve up every day.

UCHUCK III

IT'S RAINING at the head of Muchalat Inlet, which is nothing new. Dark clouds regularly crown this steep-sided fjord, which drills deep into the northwestern coast of Vancouver Island from Nootka Sound. At the inlet's edge, fourteen kilometres beyond the forest-industry town of Gold River, a gargantuan pulp and newsprint mill, now obsolete, once belched and smoked. Beside the mill, a silent Mowachaht First Nation village sleeps.

This is the terminus of Highway 28, which crosses Vancouver Island from Campbell River. A government dock eases into the water here, and beside the dock one of British Columbia's last old-time coastal freighters begins and ends its journeys. The *Uchuck III* is a throwback to the 1940s and earlier, when well-appointed steamers carried passengers, cargo and mail to a busy network of maritime communities. Industrial progress changed that way of life: refrigeration allows fishermen to bring their catch to the city for a better price; logging companies have invested in floatplanes and crew boats. But on the *Uchuck*, one can still connect with an older, slower and infinitely pleasant mode of travel that used to prevail along the British Columbia coast.

The *Uchuck III* heads through sea fog into Kyuquot Sound on a gorgeous summer morning. (ANDREW SCOTT)

The friendly crew of five—captain, mate, oiler, engineer and cook—work a regular schedule in remote Muchalat and Tahsis inlets. They deliver groceries to logging camps at Mooyah Bay, Kleeptee Creek and Plumper Harbour, drums of fuel to Houston River and Blowhole Bay, fishmeal to aquaculture stations. "Freight is how we pay the bills," explains skipper and part-owner Fred Mather, as he watches Sean Mather, his son and partner, adeptly manipulate the ship's winch and derrick to load a logging-truck engine destined for McCurdy Creek. They can manage seventy tonnes of cargo, from seedlings for tree planters to goats.

The *Uchuck* carries passengers, too. She is licensed to take one hundred people through the sheltered inlets where she mostly operates. In summer, the crew make a twice-weekly tourist run to Yuquot, a pretty Mowachaht former village site at Friendly Cove in Nootka Sound, where Captain James Cook first contacted the region's Native inhabitants. They cruise past a fishing resort located among the ruins of a cannery, check out the scenic little church at Yuquot and cross to Resolution Cove on Bligh Island, where Cook stayed for five weeks in 1778 to repair his ships. (William Bligh, who would suffer the famous mutiny later in his career as captain of the *Bounty,* was Cook's navigating officer on this trip.)

On Thursday mornings, the *Uchuck* makes the ten-hour journey to the tiny fishing village of Kyuquot, further north. This voyage involves two hours of travel off western Vancouver Island in waters notorious for their roughness and unpredictability. A different Coast Guard license is required; only a dozen passengers are permitted to throw their gear aboard—including kayaks, if they wish. The first part of the trip follows the *Uchuck*'s normal route in Muchalat and Tahsis inlets, but six kilometres before the milltown of Tahsis the boat turns west through Tahsis Narrows and Hecate Channel into Esperanza Inlet.

Esperanza is broad and long and empties into the Pacific. Despite its size, there are few human habitations there. The *Uchuck* often makes deliveries to logging camps at McBride Bay and Brodick Creek. Across the channel, tiny communities at Ceepeecee, a former cannery and reduction plant, and Esperanza, where a hospital and hotel once stood, maintain a holding action against the wilderness. Port Eliza is the last stop in the inlet, where the crew batten down the main hatch, cover it with canvas and double check the deck cargo. "We haven't missed many trips to Kyuquot," proclaims Fred Mather. "It would have to be pretty serious weather for us to turn back."

One gets a different perspective of the West Coast while bobbing offshore in the open Pacific swell. Great waves crash against rocks and cliffs, and the air is filled with salt and spray and the cries of seabirds. You get a deeper sense of the attraction that the area has for adventurers. Sometimes ghostly bands of sea mist swirl round the ship, enfolding rocks and islets in a pearly embrace and changing the view every minute. Despite having been ravaged by clearcuts, range upon receding range of green hillside pulsate with pure energy.

On the trip to Kyuquot, *Upchuck* might be a more appropriate name than *Uchuck,* which means "calm or healing waters." The forty-two-metre craft was originally the U.S. Navy minesweeper *YMS 123,* built in 1942 at North Bend, Oregon. Purchased after the war as a bare, engineless hull, she was handsomely reconditioned for coastal freighting in 1955. Some of her equipment comes from several classic B.C. steamers, including the 1903 *Princess Victoria* (steering gear and engine telegraph), the *Princess Mary* (derricks, lifeboats and rigging), the *Princess of Alberni* (winches) and a Canadian Navy frigate (anchors and ship's wheel). The gleaming diesel engines—two 500-horsepower Clevelands, which once propelled a U.S. Navy yards freighter—are presided over by engineer Bob Watson and drive the vessel along at twelve knots.

She is called *Uchuck III* because she was the third vessel with this name owned by Esson Young and George McCandless, who ran a marine service in Barkley Sound for almost two decades. In 1960, the year after the highway connecting Port Alberni with Tofino and Ucluelet was completed, Young and McCandless moved their operation north and changed its name from Barkley Sound Transportation to Nootka Sound Service. Esson's son, Dave Young, bought the business with a partner in 1979. In the mid-1990s, Nootka Sound Service was sold to its current owners.

Although the *Uchuck* operates on a regular schedule, the timetable is flexible. The boat may be waylaid by weather, for instance, or be called upon to tow a disabled pleasure boat or carry a sick logger to town. The crew may take a liking to you and detour to some favourite hideaway or stop to watch a wasplike air crane helicopter logs from nearby mountain slopes, then drop them with a gigantic splash into the inlet. Crew members combine a sound knowledge of local history with their navigating skills. They seem to know everyone on the coast and obviously enjoy their jobs. "There's always something different," says Sean Mather, scanning a river estuary with his binoculars for wildlife.

On my several voyages aboard the *Uchuck* I've seen eagles, otters, deer and seals, and watched dozens of black bears feed on crabs at low tide. Other travellers have spotted sea lions and whales. No two runs are even remotely similar. On one trip, for instance, after waiting at Kendrick Arm for a crew of tree planters, we receive a lesson in the delicate art of loading a small vessel with two heavy pickups, three men and their gear, and one dog. On the return leg a broken-down one-tonne truck has to be picked up at a precarious spot where the water is very shallow and full of rocks.

Often the *Uchuck* has kayakers aboard. On a different journey I get a chance to talk to Steve Nagode and Fred Clark from Seattle, who have been travelling mostly in Esperanza Inlet. They joined the boat at Kyuquot.

"Gale warnings three days in a row and some rough paddling," Clark tells me. "But it's a real pretty area. We saw a grey whale."

Clark and Nagode are delighted to discover they can be "wet launched" near Tahsis Narrows, only seven kilometres from the sawmill town of Tahsis where they've left their vehicle. One by one, sitting in their loaded kayaks and clutching their paddles, they're winched high in the air over the side on a wooden pallet. As the first airborne adventur-er reaches apogee, mate Glen Pollock, operating the winch, addresses him with a time-honoured question.

"How are you doing up there?" he asks. "Feeling nervous?"

"No, I'm okay," comes the predictable response.

"Well, that's good," Pollock replies, "because I've never done this before and it's sure scaring the heck out of me."

The kayak and Pollock's words dangle together in the air for a moment. Then the pallet is lowered into the water, and the relieved kayaker, his heart racing, scoots out to freedom and the long journey home.

QUEEN OF CHILLIWACK

AT SIX A.M., the *Queen of Chilliwack* slows off the derelict cannery town of Namu, 450 kilometres northwest of Vancouver. A passenger prepares to disembark. A small fishing boat appears out of the morning mist and hovers round the ferry's stern like a gnat getting ready to bite an elephant. The vehicle ramp is extended over the water, and the passenger—a cheerful, middle-aged woman of ample proportions—makes an alarming discovery: she will have to gingerly jump down from the ramp onto the deck of the bobbing gillnetter.

Whoa. BC Ferries wasn't kidding back in 1996 when it named its new route the Discovery Coast Passage. From June to September, the *Queen of Chilliwack* serves a vast, barely populated chunk of the central British Columbia coast between Port Hardy and Bella Coola. With a friendly crew, good food and coin-operated showers, the ship is unlike anything else the corporation operates. The atmosphere aboard is part modern cruise liner, part Union steamship, circa 1930. Unless you're jumping between vessels, the ferry is a delight, both for tourists and residents.

After watching our fellow traveller depart in such unexpected fashion, and then getting some breakfast, we invite

The *Queen of Chilliwack* passes Dryad Point on Campbell Island as a kayaker waits to cross Lama Passage. (ANDREW SCOTT)

ourselves up to the bridge, where it turns out Captain Don Crighton is itching for a diversion. "We thought we'd do a little gunkholing," he tells us. To "gunkhole" is a sailor's term and can be roughly translated as follows: "to explore by fecklessly squeezing a small boat into a tight place." A 115-metre ferry brings new meaning to the word. Unperturbed, Crighton steers his 5600-tonne vessel into Nalau Passage, a silent, seldom-visited body of calm water just south of Hunter Island.

"We're thinking that this might be a good place to drop off kayakers," he remarks offhandedly. Indeed, several narrow channels lead south and west to the open Pacific and a wild, little-known paddling paradise. Not far from here, white sand beaches and crashing surf line western Calvert Island and the Goose and Breadner archipelagos. All are part of Hakai Provincial Recreation Area, famous for its sportfishing, scuba diving, wildlife and First Nations history.

"You could do that?" I ask. I have a kayak strapped to the top of my car. "How would you go about it?"

"Oh, we'd just throw you off the stern and pick you up on the way back," explains Crighton, with a twinkle in his eye. I glance at Katherine, my partner. We only have one kayak, a single. We also have one vehicle, which someone will have to drive off the ferry. Well, it was a thought.

We get a chance to put in some paddling at the ferry's next two stops, McLoughlin Bay and Shearwater, which bracket the central coast's main population centre—Bella Bella—a community loosely strung out over several islands. At McLoughlin Bay on Campbell Island, which serves the First Nations side of Bella Bella, we leave the ferry for a few days and rent a wooded campsite with a view from Frank and Kathy Brown. It was here, in 1833, that the Hudson's Bay Company built one of its earliest trading posts, Fort McLoughlin, named after Dr. John McLoughlin, head of the company's West Coast operations. The fort was abandoned ten years later and no sign of it remains. As I lie in the tent at night I try to imagine how things were on this spot 160 years ago.

McLoughlin Bay is pretty quiet today. The Browns run their operation from a miniature Heiltsuk longhouse situated next to the ferry dock. An interpretive centre and gift shop, the building is set on the only purple beach I've ever seen, made from crushed sea-urchin shells, byproduct of a nearby seafood-processing plant. An ebb tide leaves the colourful spines all neatly aligned in the same direction. Frank and Kathy offer walking tours, salmon barbecues and trips in hand-decorated, fibreglass replicas of the big traditional dugout canoes that First Nations people once used for whaling and ocean travel. In more conventional craft, they'll also transport kayakers and campers to remote, outlying spots.

This first stab at tourism is an experiment for the 1800-strong Heiltsuk First Nation. Some band members feel an influx of visitors may have negative effects on their community, located three kilometres north of the ferry landing and known as Waglisla. We walk the dusty road to this big friendly village, grab a snack at the restaurant, buy a few supplies at the large co-op store and visit the tiny museum in the high school, up the street from the twenty-four-bed R.W. Large Memorial Hospital. Waglisla even has an airport, though most arrivals and departures take place at the bustling downtown dock, which points due east towards the mountains of King Island and the mainland.

From Rod and Charlotte Felton, local schoolteachers who also run a paddler-oriented guesthouse at Shearwater on neighbouring Denny Island, we rent a second kayak. This part of Bella Bella was an RCAF seaplane base in World War II; one of the aircraft hangars is still in use as a combined shipyard, store, post office, laundromat and shower. For the next few days we explore nearby waters, camping on Rainbow Island on a beautiful shingle spit with views up Seaforth Channel and Gunboat Passage. We are blessed with calm, sunny weather and see mink, sandpipers, hummingbirds, yellowlegs and sandhill cranes. Early one morning as we're making breakfast we hear a sharp exhalation—*swoosh* —quite near, and turn to find six killer whales passing our campsite.

Another day we poke along the shoreline of Campbell Island to Kynumpt Harbour, where honeysuckle vines embrace a few decaying cabins. I do a little fishing, and as I clean the catch I don't notice the incoming tide carry off my $350 graphite paddle. After a panic-fuelled forty-five-minute search using the spare paddle, I find the furtive utensil out in the middle of the bay. Tired out from all the excitement, we decide to camp there for the night. Ravens entertain us as we cook teriyaki rockfish, curried vegetables and rice for dinner.

The beauty of the mid-coast ferry route is that it opens up a part of B.C. that has been inaccessible for decades to budget travellers like us. By hopping between the various ports the ship stops at—including Klemtu, an isolated Kitasoo First Nation village, and Ocean Falls, a former pulp-and-paper metropolis, now semi-abandoned—visitors can savour the ghosts and glories of the past. This part of the coast was once a busy place, dotted with canneries, mines, modest logging operations and a much larger population than today.

The ferry cruises past the mouth of Rivers Inlet, for instance, where B.C.'s third-largest salmon fishery (after the Fraser and Skeena rivers) used to sustain eighteen canneries. Today there are only a few fishing lodges, the floating community of Dawsons Landing and the First Nation village of Owikeno at the head of the inlet. Just north of Rivers Inlet, at Safety Cove on Calvert Island, Captain George Vancouver was hoping to repair the *Chatham* when he was summoned to Nootka to negotiate with the Spanish explorer Bodega y Quadra and formalize the transfer of the northwest coast to British hands.

While the days of the handlogger and the small, independent "gyppo" contractor are long gone, the forest industry is still active on the central coast. Here, in fact, and further north are B.C.'s last great old-growth watersheds: untouched river valleys of ancient fir, spruce, cedar and hemlock. Few clearcuts are visible from the ferry's route, but the region is nevertheless under intense scrutiny from both loggers and environmentalists. The *Queen of Chilliwack* cruises right through the heart of what could become another ecological war zone, with names like Ellerslie and Koeye, now used mostly by local people to identify nearby lakes and rivers, turning into household words.

History buffs and eco-warriors, of course, are not exactly the ferry corporation's target market. Tourists, especially North Americans and Europeans, are. The *Queen* carried only 7400 passengers in 1999—fewer than a Spirit-class ship could haul between Tsawwassen and Swartz Bay in one day. The *Queen* is relatively small, however, with a crew of only twenty-six. There's capacity for 375 passengers and 132 vehicles. Passenger numbers are up from 6200 in 1996, but down from their peak of 9000 in 1998. "We're doing about as well as we expected," says Maureen Cumming, a manager with BC Ferries' corporate marketing group. "We know it's going to take some time for people to become aware of the route."

To attract travellers, the corporation has decided to focus on the details that help create a great travel experience. When was the last time you hung a fishing line off a ferry's stern, enjoyed a salmon barbecue on the top deck or played Scrabble with the kitchen crew? You can do all these things on the *Queen of Chilliwack* and watch Pacific white-sided dolphins and Dall's porpoises play off the bow, as well. If humpback or killer whales are sighted, which happens on most trips, the ferry slows or stops, and the passengers hang off the deck railings, binoculars glued to their faces, until the whales move on.

Built in Norway in 1978 as the *Basto I* and acquired by BC Ferries in 1991, the *Queen* has been refurbished twice at Victoria's Point Hope Shipyards. Driven by four six-cylinder, 1470-horsepower engines, her service speed is fourteen knots, or twenty-six kilometres per hour. The vessel has no passenger cabins. On overnight trips, travellers stretch out on reclining chairs, unroll sleeping mats or set up

tents on the outside deck. Despite these homespun arrange-
ments, it's easy to get comfortable. The galley serves up a
different fresh seafood menu every night. There's a gift
shop, and a lounge where alcohol is served. Movies and natural history videos are screened. Activities are organized for
kids, and games and books are available for borrowing.

Eventually, though, the ferry reaches the end of its journey. It makes a long eastward swing up steep-sided Dean
and Labouchere channels, passes the historic rock where
Alexander Mackenzie is believed to have marked his famous
message—"From Canada by land, 22d July 1793"—and turns
into North Bentinck Arm within sight of Bella Coola. Most
travellers leave the vessel and embark on a new adventure
here, driving across the rolling Chilcotin plateau on
Highway 20 to Williams Lake and points east.

But we decide to hang around Bella Coola, one of B.C.'s
more fascinating old villages, and explore the heritage farms
and First Nation sites of the Bella Coola valley. We talk to
the descendants of Norwegian Lutheran pioneers who settled there in the 1890s and formed, despite daunting hard-
ships, a cooperative community based on the goals of virtue
and social morality. We poke along the banks of the Bella
Coola River, where ancient grave markers moulder in the
tangled undergrowth. On the swift-moving river itself,
Nuxalk fishermen set drift nets from tiny dinghies, astonishing us with their daring. After the RVs full of German
tourists trundle off down the highway, we pretty much
have the place to ourselves.

I suspect few of those tourists know that B.C.'s first visitors to Germany came from Bella Coola. In 1885, a group of
nine Nuxalk men was hired to take part in a series of circus-
style ethnic expositions organized by Hamburg impressario
Carl Hagenbeck. They sang and danced their way across the

country for an entire year and were a great success. They adapted easily to the foreign culture, learning German, wearing smart European clothes when they weren't performing and, if contemporary reports are to be believed, acquiring European lady friends. On their safe return, one of them built a longhouse at Bella Coola topped with cedar-shingled spires and carved gargoyles, modelled after Cologne cathedral.

A surprising story, perhaps. But on the Discovery Coast, the unexpected lurks round every headland. Now that the *Queen of Chilliwack* is on the job, a thousand secret coves and channels beckon, as they did in the 1920s and '30s. The people's cruise ship is a key that unlocks the gates to a vast maritime region, a land of beauty and adventure.

Worlds Apart

THE BRITISH COLUMBIA coast has one of the world's finest selections of islands and islets, over 6000 of them, from Vancouver Island and the Queen Charlottes down to what are basically just large rocks in exposed places. I've selected only six—one one-thousandth of the total—to write about, so what follows can hardly be representative. Many of the province's larger and more populated islands are well known and have been widely described. I chose less familiar names instead.

Not all are small. Indeed, Hunter is the thirteenth largest island in B.C., while Flores ranks about thirtieth. But most are tiny places, inhabited in some cases by only a hardy handful of people. Half these islands, in fact, are no longer permanently populated. Two of them, Jedediah and Portland, are provincial marine parks, and relatively accessible (large sections of Hunter and Flores islands are preserved as parkland, too). Harwood is a Sliammon First Nation reserve. Merry Island, smallest of all, is a lighthouse station.

Islands are laboratories of change, where species diverge and evolution is accelerated. They are fragile, too, easily invaded and overrun. Life flickers out and dies there more easily than on the mainland. Islands soon develop distinct cultures and eccentricities, and B.C.'s are no exception. Life there entails a degree of emotional and physical separation.

It requires independence, determination and self-acceptance—attributes that I find exemplify the coastal culture as a whole. In a way, B.C.'s entire coastline is like one big island, with a life very much its own.

HARWOOD ISLAND

THE NORTHERN TIP of Harwood Island, a spear of white sand covered in lush, waist-high grass, looks almost tropical. The triangular spit gives Harwood its First Nations name: A'geyksn, or "pointed nose." Plunked down in the Strait of Georgia, 125 kilometres northwest of Vancouver and 5 kilometres from Powell River's steaming paper mills, A'geyksn is wild and beautiful and seldom visited. That's mainly because it's a Sliammon First Nation reserve and thus off-limits to much of the travelling public.

We arrive here with the blessings of the Sliammon people, who occupy a territory that extends from Stillwater, south of Powell River, to Desolation Sound and Cortes Island. The Sliammon speak a Salishan language; along with their neighbours, the Klahoose of Toba Inlet and the Homalco of Bute Inlet, they are the northernmost of the Coast Salish nations. Thirteen of us have kayaked over from Gibsons Beach on the mainland, three kilometres away, to partake in one of the band's new ecotourism ventures. As we bob off Harwood's gleaming strand, Murray Mitchell— or Tlex-Tan, as he's known in his own tongue—greets us in ceremonial fashion and invites us to join him on land. In no time, we're sprawled out on the shore while Murray, his wife Nancy and son Nick build a fire and show us how to barbecue salmon using traditional wood stakes and spreaders.

We all agree that this is an excellent way to spend an afternoon. A pair of bald eagles patrol the trees behind us. Puffs of scattered cloud swirl over the towering Smith and Bunster ranges to our east. Harwood's "nose" points right at Savary Island, eleven kilometres further north. Savary, Murray tells us, is Ayhus, the double-headed serpent, and this is exactly what the island looks like on a map. Ayhus fell from favour with the Transformer—that ancient, potent deity of the Coast Salish people—and was turned to stone as he tried to return to his cave at Hurtado Point near Lund. I ask Murray what role Harwood played in local myth. "This island was always here," he replies.

It was certainly here during the 9000-year sojourn of the Coast Salish. But Harwood is a fairly recent addition to the landscape, as are Savary, Hernando and Marina islands, and the southern peninsulas of Cortes and Quadra. All these places are ground-up piles of glacial clay, sand, gravel, stones and boulders. Compared to the hundred-million-year-old granite bedrock that forms much of the strait's shoreline, they are rank newcomers.

The geological processes that created Harwood are strange and wonderful. The island is part ground moraine, part outwash plain. Moraines are jumbles of rock and dirt dumped by retreating glaciers; outwash plains are formed of finer sediments dropped by glacial meltwater streams. The giant ice sheets advanced down the Strait of Georgia, faltered, then advanced again, and their deposits were shunted into heaps and bulldozed to various locations. As a result, Harwood is layered like a clubhouse sandwich. The deepest strata are known as the Cowichan Head and Semiahmoo drifts and were laid down 40 000 to 50 000 years ago. Next are the Quadra sands, thick beds of silt that date back 25 000 to 30 000 years. Above them is a mixture of clay and rock debris called Vachon till, left from the most recent glaciation and only 14 000 to 18 000 years old.

A mere 10 000 years ago, when the glaciers had fallen back to roughly their present positions, the sea level rose and the islands we see today were created. Waves and weather continue to transform Harwood, battering its slopes and ridges, stirring up sand and spreading it along the shoreline and out to sea. Sand and silt are blown to the top of the island as well, where they cover the glacial till and form the surface layer. The beach we are relaxing on, of course, with its fine, uniform grains of white feldspar, clear quartz and black hornblende, is also fashioned from this same sand.

As we wait for the fat sockeye salmon to cook, Murray and Nancy tell us how their ancestors made use of Harwood. Most Sliammon people live today in a nearby village, also called Sliammon, next to Gibsons Beach. Many of them still refer to the island as "the fridge." It was a favourite place for the men to hunt deer. They also took grouse, ducks and geese, caught fish and harpooned octopi, seals, sea lions and porpoises around the offshore reefs. The women dug clams and onion and lily bulbs, and gathered sea urchins, sea cucumbers, chitons, crabs, mussels, seagull eggs, blackberries, salal berries, huckleberries, salmonberries and fiddleheads.

Summer campsites were established on the north and south ends of the island. Some people lived year-round on Harwood, according to Murray, though well inland, in order to avoid the raiding parties of the Lekwiltok. This was a fierce, warlike nation that lived north of the Homalco and took slaves, gradually expanding its territory south through force. During the missionary era, people sometimes went to Harwood to indulge in forbidden activities such as gambling or simply to escape the presence of the black robes. The island was also a burial ground—a place, says Murray, where spirits roam.

In 1888, Indian commissioner Peter O'Reilly, accompanied by Sliammon leader Timothy Moody, toured the region and laid out reserves. The site of Sliammon was reserved first, Harwood second. O'Reilly noted that the people "cultivate small patches of land on Harwood Island," and the remains of orchards can still be seen at several locations. He reported that the island "contains 2075 acres [840 hectares], the greater portion being fairly good soil. About 50 acres [20 hectares] is open land which is used by the Indians as a run for their cattle, and sheep; the western portion is densely timbered with fir, and spruce." Captain Timothy, as Moody was known, was selling Harwood beef to local logging camps in the 1880s.

After we settle into island life, Nancy, an expert basket-maker, shows us some woven headbands and children's dolls she has crafted and brought along. She soon has half a dozen people weaving tiny medicine pouches from long strips of cedar. Murray patiently scrapes the loose fibre from a large piece of cedar bark and shows the rest of the group how to construct a traditional canoe bailer. My attention span wavers a bit when it comes to crafts, so during these demonstrations I slope off by myself and explore a little of the five-kilometre-long island.

A rusted, overgrown donkey engine and ancient truck litter the spit; beyond them, I find an old skid road that climbs Harwood's clay spine to higher ground. Red cedar, alder and bigleaf maple are the dominant species now, though dozens of big Douglas fir stumps suggest the forest looked quite different a century ago. A few days after my visit I talk to Bob de Pape, who worked on the island between 1964 and 1984. "It was all selective logging," he tells me. "We tried to keep it looking good. We took out the snags and protected the small stuff so it kept growing." Leo Johnson logged Harwood in the 1940s and 1950s; in the 1920s, it was Clay and Dewey Anderson. And there were other outfits, too, all on contract to the Sliammon band. Some didn't last long. "It was a really nice place to work," recalls de Pape. "Quiet. Nobody bothered us. We had a pretty good relationship with the band."

Even though a new contractor was working on the island just a couple of years ago, it's clear that nobody has been over my skid road in a while. The forest understorey is wall-to-wall sword fern, salal and stinging nettle. The nettles and the glutinous condition of the track force me to cut downhill to the shore, where pocket beaches alternate with accumulations of wave-smoothed boulders. (These glacial erratics surround all the Strait of Georgia's outwash islands; often they lurk just beneath the surface and make boating a perilous sport.) The sands are criss-crossed by the hoof marks of deer but, like Robinson Crusoe, not a single human footprint do I find.

I wander back to Harwood's nose in time for dinner: salmon, bannock and three types of salad. It was on this exact spot just over two centuries ago that a pair of Captain George Vancouver's officers had to make a culinary choice. Peter Puget and Joseph Whidbey were travelling with an armed crew in a small open boat, as they often did while helping make the detailed surveys that were the purpose of the journey. They camped one night on Savary Island, which they found "desirable and pleasant."

The next day they made for Harwood and were "received by a small party of Native Inhabitants, who had waded over a long Flat that extends from the Beach to meet the Boats, each having a Slice of Porpoise or Seal in their

Hands which was immediately offered to us, and though we did not accept their profer'd Generosity, yet they received an handsome present for their Good Intentions, with which they appeared highly pleased." Puget tried to persuade his new friends to take him to their village, but they "obstinately" refused, and the explorers, after gathering as many clams as they "could conveniently stow," continued on their journey.

After dinner, it's time for us to continue ours. As we pack up and paddle back, we ponder the varying outlooks of the early explorers. Vancouver was depressed by B.C.'s coastal landscape, which he termed "dreary" and "truly forlorn." He brightened a bit while approaching Harwood, as it "presented a scene more pleasing and fertile," and named the island after a Royal Navy surgeon then serving under Captain Bligh in the south Pacific.

The English crews were travelling in tandem with their Spanish counterparts, commanded by Dionisio Galiano and Cayetano Valdes, while they mapped this part of the coast. The Spaniards thought it "impossible to find a more delightful view than that which is here presented by the diversity of trees and shrubs, by the loveliness of the flowers and the beauty of the fruit, by the variety of animals and birds." For Harwood, they chose the name Isla de Concha, or Shell Island.

We wonder which of the islands in the northern strait Galiano and Valdes found the most "delightful." Savary has the best beaches, but it is subdivided today into 1700 tiny lots and has no parkland and few public facilities. Hernando is lovely, too, but is now an enclave of the super rich, lined with summer homes that wouldn't look out of place in Vancouver's Shaughnessy district. That leaves Harwood: uninhabited, undeveloped and likely to stay that way. It's little wonder the Sliammon people chose A'geyksn as one of the places they most wanted to protect.

HUNTER ISLAND

FROM OUR WILDERNESS campsite at Canal Bight, nearly 500 kilometres northwest of Vancouver, Hunter Island faces us across Lama Passage. The day is sunny and mild, but an afternoon wind has picked up, giving the water an unpleasant chop. I'm content to wait for the morning calm before kayaking this two-kilometre-wide channel, the main shipping route through the protected inland waters of B.C.'s central coast.

Through binoculars I scan the distant Hunter Island shoreline. At the beginning of World War I, a group of Icelandic immigrants came and settled on this 334-square-kilometre island's north end. They whittled homesteads from the forest, cleared fields and built a school. But by the 1930s all had left. Today I can see no sign of their efforts. The dark evergreen shores appear unaltered.

I first heard of these pioneers while researching *The Promise of Paradise*, a book I wrote about utopian communities in B.C. At the end of the nineteenth century, Scandinavian groups formed several idealistic colonies on the coast. A company of Norwegians lived at Hagensborg in the Bella Coola valley. Finnish settlers founded Sointula on Malcolm Island. On Vancouver Island, a Danish contingent chose isolated Cape Scott for its settlement, while a mixed congregation of Swedes and Norwegians ended up at Quatsino.

Besides the Hunter Island community, Icelanders estab-lished Osland, a larger settlement further north, on Smith Island near the mouth of the Skeena River. B.C.'s Icelandic pioneers had language and heritage in common, but they seemed to share no unusual ideology or beliefs. No charis-matic leaders urged them on, and so I reluctantly decided not to include their stories in the book. But I did remain curi-ous about them. And when Katherine and I get a chance to spend several weeks on the mid-coast with our kayaks one recent August, we resolve to see if anything is left of the Hunter Island settlement.

We paddle south from McLoughlin Bay on Campbell Island, former site of Fort McLoughlin, one of the earliest (1833-43) Hudson's Bay Company trading posts on the coast. BC Ferries vessels make regular stops there to serve the Heiltsuk First Nation community of Waglisla, more commonly referred to as Bella Bella. We cross over to the east side of Lama Passage and cruise along the shores of Denny Island. After about five kilometres we duck in to explore Alarm Cove, where we scare up a pair of sandhill cranes. In another five kilometres or so, we reach Canal Bight, where we camp for the night and worry unnecessarily about bears and a very high tide.

Next morning, a thick layer of fog greets us. Fortunately it is sitting about thirty metres above the waterline and no Alaska cruiseships loom out of it to threaten us as we recross Lama Passage. Soon enough we find ourselves at the north end of Hunter Island, in a maze of promontories, nooks and crannies known locally as Howyet Bay but, con-fusingly, labelled Cooper Inlet on the chart. Sunshine is breaking through as we paddle into the nook named Lizzie Cove, where there are a couple of homes, with gillnetters and trollers tied up to docks. Several spooky, derelict-looking buildings on log floats are anchored in the middle of the cove.

As kayakers, our first order of business is to find a camp-site. On B.C.'s rocky central coast, this is more difficult than one might expect. We need a flat, clear patch of land large enough for a tent and high enough to keep us dry. We must be able to haul up the boats. While the southern half of Hunter Island is parkland, part of Hakai Provincial Recreation Area, much of its northern shore is privately owned and we search in vain for an appropriate spot. Finally, in an archipelago of tiny offshore islets, we find a grassy point that would suit us perfectly. Then we paddle over to a cabin on another islet, where a man, a boy and a dog are getting ready to head off in a small boat. I ask the man if he thinks anyone would mind if we camped nearby. He identifies himself as Leo and tells us he owns the island we want to camp on. Graciously, he allows us to stay there, as long as we leave no trace. The boy tells us about a stream where we can get water. The dog wags its tail.

I ask kindly Leo if any vestiges of the Icelandic commu-nity can still be found. He ponders. In seventy years the forest has obliterated most signs of civilization. He points to yet another islet, a modest chunk of rock choked with shrubs and alders. "That's Schoolhouse Island," he says. "The settlers used to row their kids over there each morn-ing. I think the school was moved to Bella Bella around 1930." The homesteads we noted on Hunter Island are a more recent colonization, he explains. Of the earlier one, only memories remain.

The first Icelandic settler was Sam Johnson. He arrived in 1912. Then Jon Leifson came from Saskatchewan with his family, as did Halldor Fridleifson. Halldor's son, Julius, interviewed in the late 1960s for an article in a periodical called the *Icelandic Canadian,* recollected that his father "bought a 25-foot boat at Steveston, B.C. We rode it to Point Roberts where we put an engine in it and a cabin on it. That year, 1914, in May or April we left for Hunter's Island. In our boat were Halldor (Dad), Julius (myself), Gusti Iverson and a man whose name I cannot remember.

"We arrived at Howyet Bay safe and sound, after running over a log in one of the rapids on the way up there. We then built a cabin. The family came out a little later by steamboat to Bella Bella. That summer most of us went to Namu to fish or to work in the cannery. We got twelve and a half cents a sockeye salmon and two and a half for a humpback salmon there at that time. The cannery supplied the net and boat."

By 1915, about seventy people lived in the settlement. There were fifteen or twenty families, with such names as Einarson, Bjornson, Gislason, Gillis, Stefanson, Kristie, Lyngholt, Olafson, Christianson, Erlendson and Sigurdson. Old photos show them standing proudly in their homestead clearings, dressed for the occasion in their best clothes, as if to say that even here, surrounded by the forest primeval and miles from the finer things in life, they could still maintain a certain standard of dignity.

Perhaps the picturesque fjords and inlets, rich in wildlife, reminded them of their homeland. Certainly, that natural wealth kept them alive at first. They smoked and salted salmon, shot ducks and deer, grew vegetables, and eventually raised cows, chickens, pigs and goats. Supplies were ordered from Kelly Douglas and Eaton's in Vancouver and sent by steamship. In summer the men laboured at the cannery in Namu or the new pulp mill in Ocean Falls.

Others fished at Rivers Inlet or worked in logging camps. Once a week they rowed to Bella Bella for their mail.

"People were friendly and there was a lot of visiting," remembered Julius Fridleifson, "especially at our place, we being in about the centre of the settlement and being a large family. The teacher also stayed at our place. There were a few parties and some picnics, where most of us got together." Isolation and a dwindling population, though, eventually did the community in. Young people moved away to get an education or find employment. By 1923 only a few settlers remained. Soon the shores of Hunter Island were silent again.

Several families settled at Ocean Falls, where steady work and good facilities were available. Osland, the other Icelandic community, would have been an attractive destination, as well. It had a population of about ninety by the mid-1920s, plus its own school, post office, store, Farmer's Institute and marine fuel station. This village was founded in 1913 by a group from Manitoba after an abortive attempt to form a colony on the Queen Charlotte Islands. Osland's residents tried to preserve elements of their ethnic heritage by teaching *glima*, or Icelandic wrestling, and building up an Icelandic-language library. Attempts to grow fruit and raise mink for fur were unsuccessful, but fishing and hunting kept the place alive until World War II, after which many people moved to Prince Rupert. Now, only a few summer homes remain at the site.

We spend the night on Leo's island, camped on a resilient layer of yarrow, springbank clover, red paintbrush and silverweed. Next day, we paddle into Fannie Cove, next door to Lizzie Cove, where the Icelanders had also settled, to pump crystal water from a pretty creek that drains Hunter Island's hilly core. The mouth of Fannie Creek is part of a Heiltsuk reserve. "Some of the Indians from Bella Bella would come in the fall," recalled Fridleifson, "to fish in the bay and smoke or dry their salmon in shacks which they had at the head of the inlet. Sam Johnson took pictures of them quite often, and once in a while they would come to get milk for their babies after we got the cows. Otherwise there was little or no fraternization with them."

As we explore Hunter Island's shorelines, looking for nonexistent signs of the Icelandic colony, we find perfect grass circles that can only have been made by sleeping deer. Ravens, kingfishers and bald eagles fly overhead. A small pod of harbour porpoises forages in one of the bays. We see a family of otters at play. A lone mink watches us cautiously. Under clear blue skies, we reflect on another of Fridleifson's recollections. "Life on the island for us was rather pleasant and varied," he reported. We can only agree.

FLORES ISLAND

THE BRUSH BEHIND Whitesand Cove forms a seamless wall of salal, alder and evergreen huckleberry. Further in, it's spruce and cedar. The two-kilometre-long beach is misnamed; the sand is golden grey, not white. We're looking for the path to some sulphur springs, which should start around here, according to our map. And there's a hanging net float, common trailhead sign. We stare at the vegetation from a distance of about five metres, but it's clear: there is no entrance. This stuff is impenetrable. We ask the only other people camping nearby about the supposed trail. They couldn't find it, either. Well that's the way it is with maps, we say. Sometimes they're wrong.

At the end of the beach, there is definitely a trail—and a wonderful wooden sign, illustrated with two shamanistic figures praying on either side of a winged being. "Kwaatswiis," the sign reads. "Histories of Young Indian Doctor." This is all a mystery to us, but we plunge down the path anyway, hoping it will lead us to the aforementioned springs. But the route skips round a headland and spits us out at the edge of the next bay. It also has a gorgeous gold-grey strand.

We're on Flores, a 155-square-kilometre island halfway down the west coast of Vancouver Island in Clayoquot

Wilderness adventurers are welcome to use the old search-and-rescue cabin near Cow Bay on Flores Island. (ANDREW SCOTT)

Sound. Flores is relatively flat where it faces the open Pacific, and the thick-forested southwest coast is fringed with beach after beach. The northern end of the island is mountainous. We're beyond the reach of the provincial highway network here. But we're still part of the park system, thankfully. The island is ideal for camping. In summer, when the weather normally cooperates, most people get here by kayak. Five of us, friends from the Sunshine Coast, have stuffed a week's worth of supplies and gear into our fragile fibreglass shells and paddled across the sound from the cheerful village of Tofino, sixteen kilometres to the southeast.

As we float along enjoying the scenery, I reflect that many people fought for a long time to preserve the forests that surround us. From my vantage point in Calmus Passage, I could almost be forgiven for thinking they had succeeded: the mountain slopes look mostly unscarred.

From other vantage points, in other parts of the sound, there are clearcuts aplenty. The name Clayoquot became synonymous with environmental crusading in the 1980s and early 1990s. Battles over logging in the last of Vancouver Island's old-growth watersheds, six of which are located in Clayoquot, culminated in 1993 with a summer of civil disobedience. Almost a thousand protesters were arrested. A controversial land-use decision was finally made: one-third of the area would be protected, three-quarters of the productive ancient forest could still be logged.

The late July weather turns out perfect for paddling: low overcast in the morning with calm waters, clearing to windy, sun-dazzled afternoons and evenings. We cross Heynen and Father Charles channels on our first day, skirting the northeast coast of Vargas Island, and camp for the night at Milties, a small beach well away from the open ocean. Vargas, like Flores, was named by colonial Spanish explorers for officials in Spain's great empire. Like Flores, its western shores are also encrusted with stupendous beaches. Milties is a staging point; many paddlers stay there on their first or last day out. Five days from now, when we stop here again on our return journey, a grey whale will be feeding in the bay right in front of our campsite.

While all concerned argue over how Clayoquot's forests should be cut, industrial activity has slumped and tourism bloomed. As we eat our dinner of chicken tacos, boatload after boatload of survival-suited whale-watchers zoom by our beach and roar into the distance, heading to the whale feeding grounds. Throughout the sound, dozens of other kayakers are camped for the evening and marvelling at their good fortune. Tofino is abustle. Travellers, young and old, are arriving from all over the world for the dramatic surf, glistening sands, wildlife and blue-green views.

In 1999, an agreement between forestry giant MacMillan Bloedel, the Nuu-chah-nulth First Nations and four major environmental groups was announced. A new company, Iisaak, jointly owned by MacBlo and the Nuu-chah-nulth, would do some small-scale, eco-certified logging, but not in the intact old-growth valleys. The environmentalists would endorse the operation. One local group, the Friends of Clayoquot Sound, who seek an end to all old-growth logging, refused to sign. Interfor, another big forest company with a right to log in the sound, chose to go their own way and rolled out an alternative five-year plan for eighty-three clearcuts.

On our second morning, we paddle round to the scary side of Vargas—a succession of beaches and reefs that take a regular pounding from the full Pacific swells. In certain sheltered coves, where we can avoid landing in surf, we get out for short but sensational hikes along the shore. As the clouds melt away and the wind picks up, we retreat back to Milties for the night. It's tofu stir-fry this evening, my turn to cook. We sip merlot and gaze out directly at the Catface Range on the mainland. Interfor has proposed ten cutblocks for this peninsula. Four have been approved already. Road-building can start any time. Neither logging nor protesting had taken place there at the end of 1999, six months after our visit. Instead, an uneasy stalemate prevails, with Interfor and its opponents both poised for immediate action.

The weather holds, and we make a morning crossing to Flores Island and Whitesand Cove, our home for the next three days. We soon discover that the mysterious path with the strange painted sign is actually the Wild Side Trail, built in 1996 as a joint initiative by the Nuu-chah-nulth people of Ahousat and the Western Canada Wilderness Committee. Eleven kilometres long, the route links Ahousat, the only community on Flores, to half a dozen idyllic beaches, ending at Cow Bay where another, rougher trail leads up 902-metre Mount Flores. Every kilometre or so, a sign denotes some aspect of local culture and refers visitors to a heritage trail booklet for more information.

We'll soon reach Ahousat, we realize, so we decide to look for the springs another day. The village is a pretty relaxed place, with a fine setting, perched on a narrow isthmus between Millar Channel and Matilda Inlet. On the channel side, naturally, there's an excellent sand beach. On the inlet side, a wharf juts out into a completely protected boat anchorage. Ahousat has the charm of a place that cannot be reached by automobile; footpaths and boardwalks connect the scattered homes, and nothing is built in rows.

The people are welcoming and gentle. It's hard to imagine that, in 1864, a group of Nuu-chah-nulth men, driven to desperate measures by the illegal activities of whiskey traders, burned the *Kingfisher* in Matilda Inlet and killed its four-man crew. British warships were despatched from Esquimalt to shell and burn the village and punish the culprits. Eleven prisoners, taken for trial to Victoria, were acquitted for lack of evidence. Their leader was never captured. Solid, cast-iron projectiles are still found buried in the area.

A cannonball would make a dramatic souvenir, but we search instead for a Wild Side booklet. At the store, phone calls are made, and the author, seventy-one-year-old Stanley Sam, Sr., tracks us down as we wander about. He explains that the trail was used by the Nuu-chah-nulth for ages, but became overgrown and muddy. Twenty young people did the restoration work, building three kilometres of boardwalk to protect fragile sections. Sam provided stories about significant spots along the route—places like K'iihxnit, home to a spiritual octopus; Tl'atl'athinkwuu'is, where sea serpents slid down sand dunes; and Katkwuuwis, a grisly execution site from the early 1800s, when two Nuu-chah-nulth groups, the Ahousahts and the Otsosahts, were engaged in bitter warfare. The stories became the basis for the signs and the booklet.

Over the next few days we explore the Wild Side by foot and kayak. We discover bucolic rivers meandering down to the sea, old search-and-rescue cabins that anyone can use and, of course, beach after beach. Some of us spy the far-off spouting of whales. One morning I pass the net float hung on Whitesand beach—the trailhead marker with no trail—and decide to walk closer. At a distance of two metres, the bush reconstitutes itself like one of those art-works you move in front of your eyes until it reveals a three-dimensional scene. What is revealed here is a subtle entrance into the forest that angles away from the beach.

Shortly thereafter, with companion and bathing materials in tow, I pass through this portal. Towering conifers soon give way to stunted trees and, eventually, to a swampy terrain dominated by peat moss. The trail becomes a series of loose boards and chunks of wood and stepping stones thrown down in the mud. Unusual plants begin to catch our eye: aromatic sweet gale, slender bog orchid, running clubmoss and a tiny insect-eating species, the round-leaved sundew.

We finally reach Matilda Inlet and find the sulphur springs. The water runs through an old concrete tub, two metres wide and six metres long. Two couples from nearby anchored yachts are already there, staring doubtfully at this setup. It looks clean enough to us, though, so when the yachties finally leave we have ecobaths. We take turns soaping up at the edge of the tub and using a handy clam shell to splash water over each other for rinsing off. And then—eeeaaaghh—we hop in. At a steady 23° Celsius, this water is cool compared to the popular Ramsay thermal pools at Hot Springs Cove further west. But the experience is like Clayoquot itself: the longer we immerse ourselves, sur-rounded by forest and sea, the better we feel.

JEDEDIAH ISLAND

FROM SECRET COVE, on the Sunshine Coast north-west of Vancouver, it's an easy twelve-kilometre run across Malaspina Strait to Upwood Point, the southern tip of Texada Island. Our neighbours, Ron and Carolyne Breadner, have invited us out for a jaunt in the *Squitty*, their eight-metre powerboat. It's a glorious spring day. The sky is robin's-egg blue, the air crisp. Our quest is to check out a recently acquired jewel in British Columbia's marine park system: 243-hectare Jedediah Island, just west of Texada.

As we round Upwood Point, the breeze freshens. There are whitecaps on Sabine Channel, which separates Texada and Lasqueti islands and acts as a funnel for the Strait of Georgia's prevailing northwest and southeast winds. Jedediah is dead ahead, its rocky bluffs visible behind a cluster of smaller islands. Stuck out in the middle of a channel that is itself stuck out in the middle of a strait, this tiny archipelago has the feel of true wilderness.

Jedediah may be isolated but its wildness has been tempered by a domestic quality. The island was the site of a farm for more than a hundred years. As we head out of the wind and inch cautiously into the shallow waters of Home Bay, the weathered farmhouse comes into view. Built by the

The old farmhouse on Jedediah Island, built in 1907 by the Foote family, was occupied until the early 1990s. (KATHERINE JOHNSTON)

Foote family of Vancouver in 1907 and occupied by a succession of owners until the early 1990s, the building has been sealed off by BC Parks until its future is decided. You can peer through the windows at the old kitchen stove. Work tools still hang in the shed. Rusting farm machinery quietly disintegrates in the fields.

Jedediah was named in 1860 by Captain G.H. Richards, who surveyed much of the B.C. coast. Richards decided to honour his rather obscure friend, Jedediah Stevens Tucker, son of a secretary to a British admiral. Perhaps he was running low on relevant place names at the time. The first land grant on the island was issued about 1885. Harry Foote purchased Jedediah in 1890, and he and his family used it as a recreational retreat and hobby farm for three decades. Henry and Jenny Hughes were the next owners, and they lived there full-time for many years before selling it to the Shaw family.

Mary Palmer and her first husband, Ed Mattice, bought the island from the Shaws in 1949. The couple owned a plant nursery in Seattle; Mary also worked as the gardening editor of the *Seattle Post-Intelligencer*. They treated Jedediah as a summer camp for a few years, then sold the nursery business and moved there permanently. The sale didn't work out, however, and neither did the marriage. They divorced, Ed getting the nursery and Mary the island. She moved back to Seattle to work and raise her two boys, while caretakers looked after Jedediah.

It was not until 1971 that she was able to return. She had remarried in the interim, and Mary and her new husband, Al Palmer, decided to farm Jedediah seriously, raising sheep and other livestock and growing vegetables and fruit. Their pioneer existence had many discomforts and inconveniences, but they stayed until the early 1990s. The Palmers never let their seclusion get them down; instead, they delighted in company and in visiting the area's other homesteaders. Mary wrote a chronicle of her time there, *Jedediah Days*, a tribute to good neighbours, cooperation, kindness and homegrown entertainments.

When Mary and Al announced in 1994 that they planned to sell Jedediah, the property became the focus of an intense fundraising and lobbying campaign. It was offered to the province for $4.2 million, well below market value, but the government said it had no money for such a purchase. The Friends of Jedediah, a group of local citizens, mostly from Lasqueti, swung into action to find alternative funding and get the island protected as a park.

The estate of Dan Culver, a local outdoorsman and jour-nalist who died in 1993 descending K2, the world's second-highest mountain, contributed $1.1 million to this campaign. Hundreds of individuals and groups, including Mountain

Equipment Co-op and the Nature Trust of B.C., gave another $500 000. The Pacific Marine Heritage Legacy, a joint initiative of the federal and provincial governments, provided $2.6 million. And in March 1995, the island was reborn as a provincial park. In 1997, nearby Jervis and Bunny islands were also preserved as parkland.

We're grateful to be arriving at Jedediah in the comfort of the *Squitty;* we'd be hard-pressed to reach it otherwise. Although we have Home Bay to ourselves this early in the season, more than 2000 vessels and about 7000 individuals will visit the island over the course of the year. Roughly half will come in yachts; another 35 percent or so by power craft. The rest, presuming no one drops by on an inner tube or raft, will likely be in kayaks and canoes. All the larger islands in Sabine Channel—including Jedediah, Paul, Bull, Rabbit and Jervis—boast secluded coves and plenty of pocket beaches. Perfect for paddling, provided you can solve the problem of getting there, from Lasqueti or Texada or the mainland.

The part of Jedediah around the old farmstead, where twenty fairly flat hectares have been cleared and converted to meadow and orchard, feels like a postcard from the past, freeze-dried and suspended in time. As we wander through the fields, we find it easy to imagine that the owners have just slipped away for a moment and will soon be back. Will, a shaggy old horse who lives on Jedediah, enhances the illusion by ambling over in search of a snack, then following us around with his nose in our backpacks. He seems lonely there. God knows, the sixty or seventy skittish sheep we see lurking in the woods can't be much company. Two dozen feral goats, probably the descendants of animals introduced over a century ago, also survive.

What will happen to these creatures—and to Jedediah itself—in the future? Parks officials have been working with

the Friends of Jedediah and other interested parties, including Al and Mary Palmer and the Culver family, to craft a
management strategy for the island. "People are pleased
we're involving them," says parks planner Kris Kennett.
"There's a lot of really positive energy around Jedediah."

Nearly everyone involved wants to see the island's original Douglas fir and arbutus ecosystem restored. This type
of landscape is found only in the highly urban southwestern
corner of B.C. and is poorly represented in the province's
parks inventory. The feral sheep and goats, says Kennett,
are disrupting the system with their incessant nibbling, so
new homes will have to be found for them. Few
wildflowers, for instance, survive on Jedediah, even though
the livestock-free surrounding islands are loaded with them.

The old farmhouse will be preserved temporarily in the
hope that a private society can raise the funds necessary for
its permanent protection. If those funds are not forthcom-
ing, it will probably be dismantled, as will an unfinished
building at Long Bay. A small dock or float is planned for
Home Bay, not for moorage but to improve access for the
elderly and handicapped. The meadow will be mowed occasionally. Rock cairns with commemorative plaques have
been built in front of the farmhouse to honour Al and Mary
Palmer and Dan Culver. But apart from these minor alter-
ations, Jedediah will be allowed to revert to its natural state.

As we proceed on our tour, we craft our own strategy
for enjoying this fading fragment of history on future visits.
For longer stays, Jedediah has some good campsites—especially at Sunset Cove and at Sand Beach on Home Bay—
though no ready drinking water. The island is a delight for
rambling. Pleasant trails criss-cross from Home and Codfish
bays on the east shore to Deep, Boom and Long bays on the
west, and also lead up to 200-metre Gibraltar, the island's

high point. The paths wind through a sixty-year-old second-growth forest of Douglas fir, grand fir and red cedar that covers much of the property.

Salal, Oregon grape and sword fern occupy the forest understorey, while groves of lodgepole pine and ancient Douglas fir inhabit dry upper slopes and rocky areas. Sunny headlands are home to arbutus, Rocky Mountain juniper and prickly-pear cactus. Black-tailed deer, raccoons, mink, river otters and small rodents all live on Jedediah. Birds are abundant: screech owls and woodpeckers nest in tree cavities; bald eagles, osprey and turkey vultures hover overhead; songbirds flourish in the forests; seabirds patrol the shorelines. Tidal pools and offshore areas are rich in marine life.

Even though BC Parks considers old Will a "liability problem" due to his occasional bouts of aggression, he will remain at the farm for the rest of his days. Give him a light swat on the nose if his demands for food become too pressing. But don't forget to pack him an apple or two when you go.

PORTLAND ISLAND

IF MAJOR-GENERAL Frank "One-Arm" Sutton had realized his dream, we would probably not be closing in on Portland Island today by kayak. Sutton planned to build a golf course, a luxury hotel and 200 resort cottages on his property and offer his guests the best pheasant shooting in the British Empire. It's unlikely that sweaty paddlers would have been greeted with open arms. Fortunately, the general's vision was supplanted by a broader, more democratic one; this Gulf Islands jewel has been transformed into Princess Margaret Provincial Marine Park. Once it was the plaything of freewheeling capitalists. Now anyone can drop by.

We paddle over from Saanich Peninsula, four kilometres to the south, wending through the archipelago that protects the BC Ferries terminal at Swartz Bay. It's a bit unnerving to be so close to the huge vessels, but we approach the park through Stranger Pass, which separates two beautifully tended private islands, Knapp and Pym, and is too shallow for ferries. Then we cross Shute Passage—wide and deep but rarely used by commercial traffic. Princess Margaret is popular with boaters, who can anchor safely in its protected bays and then amble ashore to stretch their legs or have a picnic. Paddlers like ourselves are rewarded for their efforts with campsites set in lovely shoreline groves of arbutus, Douglas fir and wild rose. The park even attracts divers, who can check out the *G.B. Church*, a coastal freighter that was sunk offshore in 1991 by the Artificial Reef Society of B.C.

Many visitors are content to laze around the island's edges, but we head inland, as well, to listen for whispers and echoes of Portland's curious past. The island was named after the flagship of Rear Admiral Sir Fairfax Moresby, commander of Britain's north Pacific fleet from 1850 to 1853 and based in Esquimalt. Substantial middens, or shell refuse sites, suggest that the Coast Salish First Nation people had summer fishing camps here, though a permanent village seems never to have been established. The first settlers were Kanakas—immigrants from the Sandwich Islands, as Hawaii was known in the nineteenth century.

A number of Kanakas came to the Pacific Northwest in the mid-1800s and worked for the Hudson's Bay Company. William Naukana, who had a long career in the region, eventually pre-empted most of Portland in 1875, along with his son-in-law John Palua. They moved onto the island with their large families and with other Kanakas, who may have worked for them. Early homesteaders, they cleared about forty hectares of forest, raised sheep and cattle, planted orchards and vegetable gardens and operated a primitive ferry service, hauling people and freight around the Gulf Islands in a canoe. Naukana sold the island in 1907, the year of Palua's death, and moved to nearby Saltspring along with many members of his extended family. Today, Kanaka Bluff on the southwest corner of the island and the tiny Pellow Islets (another spelling for Palua) off the northeast coast commemorate these rugged pioneers.

Portland Island's twentieth-century owners spent little time there. Instead, a series of tenant farmers continued to clear land and raise crops and animals. Today, the clearings are reverting back to forest. The remaining farm buildings, sadly vandalized, were dismantled in the late 1980s. But there are still many quiet meadows to explore. A few years ago, observant visitors might even have spotted one of the island's last sheep, quite wild by then, peering from the bushes. (At one point, the parks ministry installed a professional shep- herd to look after the proliferating beasts, but later decided to round them up and remove them because of the damage they did to plant life. A few elderly rams eluded capture, but BC Parks area supervisor Bob Austad says they haven't been seen now for a couple of years and have probably all expired.)

Island wanderers are more likely to see black-tailed deer, raccoons and mink than feral sheep. At Princess Bay, a well-used anchorage at the south end of Portland, we watch as a family of river otters catch sculpins at dusk, then rest on their backs to eat them. Black oystercatchers, gulls, ducks, murres, great blue herons, kingfishers, sandpipers and crows patrol the shores, while bald eagles, turkey vultures and the occasional osprey wheel overhead. Tidal pools are bright with starfish and anemones. Colonies of harbour seals occupy the offshore rocks.

We check out several lovely campsites on Portland. The one between Shell Beach and Kanaka Bluff has picnic tables and a great sunset. To the north, Arbutus Point has a white shell strand—and an equally fine sunrise. We settle instead beside a tiny cove on the west shore, where we can look out over Satellite Channel and watch the illuminated ferries go by at night.

Our days are spent circumnavigating the 194-hectare island by kayak and on foot. Excellent trails follow the shore- line and also cross Portland north to south and east to west, tunnelling through the salal and arbutus and over the thick moss. The climate here is dry; located in the rain shadow of Vancouver Island and the Olympic Mountains, the island receives over 2300 hours of sun a year and only seventy-five centimetres of the wet stuff. Garry oak, Rocky Mountain juniper and yellow-flowered prickly-pear inhabit the rocky coast. Spring visitors will find showy white fawn and chocolate lilies, blue camas, sea blush, harvest brodiaea and blue-eyed mary. A few species introduced by early settlers still flourish, especially the apple and plum trees in the orchard next to Princess Bay.

By 1911, ownership of Portland Island had passed from author and poet Sir Clive Phillips-Woolley to "noted seed-grower" T.H. Simpson, to Charles Davenport Taylor, a wealthy businessman, who transported guests to his property aboard the *Anemone II*, a splendid yacht. Taylor had a keen eye for development and planned to create a stylish resort there, but his scheme came to an abrupt, mysterious halt and the island was sold.

Portland's most peculiar owner, a freelance British engineer and inventor named Frank Sutton, showed up in 1927. One-Arm Sutton was notorious. He had lost a limb at Gallipoli but still golfed to an eleven-handicap. He had built railroads in Argentina and gold mines in Siberia. His specialty, however, was providing military assistance to ambitious generals. He helped Manchurian warlord Chang Tso-lin gain control over half of China, became a general himself and raked in a 3 percent royalty on all the munitions he could manufacture. Then he grew fascinated with racehorses.

After a huge sweepstake win, Sutton arrived in Vancouver with an estimated £500 000 and started spreading it around. He bought land and mining claims near Barkerville, buildings in downtown Vancouver and Shaughnessy, cars and boats and planes—and Portland Island, for which he paid $40 000.

His lifestyle, needless to say, was flamboyant, and the news-papers hung on his every word. He promoted an impractical plan for a Peace River railroad and prepared to run for parliament. Then the Great Depression intervened.

Sutton was not the kind of guy to let a little stock-market collapse slow him down. On Portland, in addition to a golf course and hotel, he designed lavish yachting and bathing facilities and prepared to raise 2000 pheasants. He bought dozens of racehorses, converted the island's main barn to a stable and laid out a racecourse. But his business ventures were foundering. Income failed to cover debt pay-ments, and he crept to the brink of bankruptcy. By 1933, having either lost or been forced to dispose of everything he owned, he had returned to China with a scheme for selling armoured vehicles to Chiang Kai-shek. Portland Island had escaped. Its bucolic existence resumed.

Portland's last owners were retired U.S. diplomat William Leander Lee Barker, who may have known Sutton in Asia, and Saltspring entrepreneur Gavin Mouat. In 1958, Mouat traded the property to the B.C. government for log-ging rights elsewhere, and three months later, Premier W.A.C. Bennett gave Portland to Princess Margaret while she was visiting. The idea was that she would donate the property as a park, which would be named for her, but after she accepted the deed, nothing happened. Protocol broke down and everyone was confused. Who should call whom? Four years later, by which time outdoors club members were writing embarrassing letters to Her Highness, royal assent was secured. The park didn't open until late 1967.

We're fortunate that this idyllic spot is part of the public realm. Paddlers have dozens of nooks and crannies to explore. Hikers can wander the pretty trails and boaters take refuge in calm harbours. The island may seem a world away, but it's actually quite close to civilization and easy enough to get to with a small boat. Just don't imitate the example of One-Arm Sutton, who pioneered an alternative method of reaching Portland that is frowned upon today. When the captain of a passing CPR steamship refused to stop and let him off at his property, Frank jumped into the water and swam ashore.

MERRY ISLAND

EVERY FIFTEEN SECONDS, all night long, a faint pattern of light moves across my bedroom wall. It's the beacon from the Merry Island lighthouse, five kilometres away. The repetition is soothing: a slow heartbeat, a reminder that all is well. From the safety of my bed I think about danger on dark, raging seas, about being lost, or injured, or broken down. Any lighthouse beam would be welcome, surely, its signal of potential assistance like a handshake across the water. Indeed, keepers from Merry Island have been watching over the Strait of Georgia for ninety-seven years. Two years ago, that vigil nearly ended.

The lighthouse, north of Nanaimo and a few kilometres west of Sechelt, is in a strategic location. It marks the entrance to Welcome Passage, a sheltered channel that offers respite from open water in rough weather. It also alerts mariners that the broad reach of the strait is interrupted here by dangerous obstructions. Two well-known tugs, the *Commodore Straits* and the *Lornet,* rest beneath infamous Fraser Rock, as does the *Tahsis III,* a barge fashioned from the hull of the *Princess Victoria,* a former Canadian Pacific steamship. Another tug, *Salvage Chief,* and two smaller wrecks attract divers to a reef due south of the lighthouse, where author Betty Pratt-Johnson

The gardening skills of keeper Kathy Richards have coaxed spring flowers from the rocks. (ANDREW SCOTT)

says the visibility is the best she has seen outside the tropics.

Named after a nineteenth-century iron merchant and racehorse owner, Merry Island is a mere kilometre long and 300 metres wide, about twenty-two hectares in surface area. When a heavy rain falls, it's just a vague forested blob on the horizon. Sometimes a swirling sea-fog snuffs out its silhouette entirely. But on sunny days the island positively glows. The whitewashed, red-roofed buildings perched on its southern tip blaze like tiny gemstones. I often stare at them from the kitchen window and wonder what it would be like to live there.

So, when Katherine and I are invited to join a grade 4 class from the local elementary school for a visit to the station, we jump at the chance. The *Lindsay*, a powerful RCMP catamaran that throws up a great roostertail of spray as it travels, takes time from fighting crime to pick everyone up at Halfmoon Bay's government wharf and whisk us across the channel. We are off-loaded by rubber inflatable and deposited in groups at the Merry Island boat ramp, where the bearded, jovial lightkeeper greets his latest visitors.

Don Richards, assisted by his wife Kathy, has been keeper at Merry Island since 1986. Their son Adam, now nineteen, grew up there, commuting to high school in Sechelt each weekday via boat. Only severe weather would prevent Adam from crossing over to the mainland, and he rarely missed more than a few days of school each year as a result of his unusual lifestyle. By all accounts outgoing and articulate—and quite unlike the stereotype of the shy lighthouse kid—Adam has a great love of theatre and acting that he hopes to develop as he pursues a university education.

Merry Island is not a hardship post, like some of British Columbia's island lights. Water must be collected in cisterns, but the station has hydro, and the delights of civilization are close by. A gleaming red and white Coast Guard supply ship, the *Sir Wilfrid Laurier*, shows up regularly. Lightkeeping duties are shared with an assistant, Rod Tainio, who maintains a separate bachelor household. The residences are small and plain, but come with million-dollar views, especially of storms. In a good southwesterly, "the windows bend right in," says Kathy. "We can hardly talk."

The Richards were posted at more exposed stations earlier in Don's career: Carmanah Point and Pachena Point on the west coast of Vancouver Island and Lucy Island in Chatham Sound. Lucy, in particular, has an isolated feel, though it's only twenty kilometres west of Prince Rupert. When I visited on a kayaking trip, its loneliness was heightened by the fact that it had recently been automated, its keepers sent elsewhere.

Some of the province's island stations can be downright dangerous places to work. The Pine Island light, stuck out in the entrance to Queen Charlotte Sound, was nearly obliterated by a seventeen-metre-tall rogue wave in 1967. Pendril Brown and his family escaped danger but were forced to pass a cold, wet night outside. Further north, the Egg Island light was wiped out by a tsunami in 1948. Keeper T.R. Wilkins, his wife and ten-year-old son spent five miserable days in their pyjamas, without food, water or shelter, and were suffering badly from exposure when finally rescued.

Triple Island, or "Little Alcatraz," forty-five kilometres west of Prince Rupert, was a particularly forbidding place to work before the days of radio, especially in winter. When Thomas Watkins, the first keeper, became ill in January 1923, his wife hung a flag at halfmast and prayed for a vessel to pass by. None did and Watkins died. There was nowhere to bury him, so the poor woman and her daughters dragged the corpse onto the station roof, where it froze in a shroud of sea ice. When help finally arrived a week later, the cadaver had to be chipped out before it could be taken away.

Merry Island has seen its own portion of tragedy: radio operator Gerald Pike was burned to death in 1927 after accidentally igniting a can of gasoline. But today, as youngsters swarm over the grounds, the scene is idyllic. Kathy shows us her garden of daffodils, tulips and grape hyacinths, carefully planted in sheltered hollows in the rock that she has filled with imported soil. Don Richards takes groups of students to inspect the weather office. The walls inside are papered with meteorological aids: maps, cloud charts, landform profiles for gauging distance and cloud height, a Beaufort wind scale (maximum force noted at the station: 133 kilometres per hour).

The keepers spend much of their time there, he explains, filing marine reports every three hours and aviation reports four times a day. They measure wind speed and direction, rainfall, temperature and atmospheric pressure. They report on visibility, sea state and sky condition. The sun's rays are monitored by a glass sphere, which burns a record of solar activity onto a piece of cardboard and confirms the right of this region to call itself the Sunshine Coast. The Merry Island station fills an important niche in B.C.'s weather-watching system, which is probably the main reason it has lasted as long as it has before being scheduled for automation.

Despite a tidal wave of public outrage and dismay, the Coast Guard automated eight B.C. lighthouses in 1996 and 1997. Groups as varied as the B.C. Aviation Council and the Coastal Communities Network argued that the new technologies being installed would cost more and be far less reliable than the men and women they were replacing. They could not help in marine emergencies. Although plans to "destaff" twenty-seven more West Coast lights, including Merry Island, were postponed in 1998, the federal government has made it clear that it will keep trying to whittle away at Canada's lightkeeping tradition and dismantle century-old heritage lighthouse structures wherever it sees an opportunity to do so.

After our station tour, we join the children for a walk to some high, mossy bluffs, which are covered this sunny spring day with pink sea blush, blue camas and yellow monkeyflowers. Many lily and orchid species flourish on the island, along with saskatoon berries, juniper, bitter cherry, arbutus and an unusual thicket of trembling aspen, which is uncommon on the B.C. coast and likely grew from a single plant that spread by putting out suckers. We spot seals on offshore rocks, and hundreds of ducks.

Except for the two-hectare portion used for the lighthouse station, Merry Island is in private hands today. Will

Franklin, the first keeper, was the original owner of the property. He manned the light from 1903 until 1932, then stayed on the island, tending his garden and an assortment of sheep, ducks and chickens, for another twenty-one years. His overgrown, spooky old home still stands, as do several other buildings. Franklin's second wife sold Merry Island in 1954, and it is now owned by two Vancouver families.

In the early days, the keepers' duties often included dangerous rescue missions. Will Franklin saved more than a few lives, and the exploits of a later keeper, George Potts, who plucked several boat crews off nearby reefs, were celebrated by Coast Guard officials and the press. Don Richards has been present at a number of accidents, including one where a cabin cruiser ran out of fuel during a night storm and almost got blown onto the rocks in front of the station. Even the keepers can run into trouble. Kathy Richards and Rod Tainio were returning home from the mainland in April 1999, when their outboard stalled and then caught fire. Flames rapidly engulfed the fibreglass vessel, and the duo were forced to abandon ship and spend a life-threatening twenty minutes in the cold water before being rescued. The burning hulk drifted in Halfmoon Bay for hours.

This year may be the Richards' last on the lights, as Don hopes to take early retirement soon. When the Richards do retire, those of us who live within view of Merry Island hope the Coast Guard won't shut the station down. The island light, while not as powerful as the one that shone a few years ago, still tracks across our bedroom walls. The mournful foghorn, which the government has already applied to remove, still sounds. For now, the station survives, an icon of uncertainty. With its strong links to the past and its fragile, unpredictable future, the outpost aptly reflects the condition of the British Columbia coast and all who live there.

Index

ABOUT
THE AUTHOR

Andrew Scott's work has appeared in *Equinox*, *Discovery*, *Big Picture*, *Islands*, *Endless Vacation*, *enRoute*, *Vancouver*, *Beautiful British Columbia*, *The Toronto Star* and dozens of other magazines and newspapers in Canada, the U.S., Hong Kong, Australia and New Zealand. He is a former editor-in-chief of *Western Living* magazine, senior editor of the *Globe & Mail*'s city magazine network (*WEST, Toronto* and *Montreal*) and publisher of *Alaska Airlines Magazine*. He has received a National Magazine Gold Award for personal journalism, and four Western Magazine Awards, including one for best article from British Columbia. He writes a monthly column about the B.C. coast for *The Georgia Straight* and recently served as a senior editor for *The Encyclopedia of British Columbia*. His first book was *The Promise of Paradise: Utopian Communities in B.C.* Scott lives in Halfmoon Bay on B.C.'s Sunshine Coast.